Fraud of the Century

Fraud of the Century

THE CASE OF THE
MYSTERIOUS SUPERTANKER SALEM

Arthur Jay Klinghoffer

Routledge
London

First published in 1988 by
Routledge
11 New Fetter Lane, London EC4P 4EE

Set in Century Schoolbook 10/11pt.
by Columns
and printed in Great Britain
by Richard Clay Ltd, Chichester, Sussex

British Library Cataloguing in Publication Data
Klinghoffer, Arthur Jay
  Fraud of the century: the case of the
  mysterious supertanker Salem.
  1. Fraud   2. Shipping
  I. Title
  364.1'63   HV6691
  ISBN 0-415-00246-X

To Judy and Joella

Who did not temporize or criticize
and gracefully accepted being Anglicized
without becoming exercised

■ Contents

▌Acknowledgments

▪ Research for this book began in the United States, but was then continued and completed in London where I resided for a most intellectually stimulating and productive year. I would like to thank Rutgers University for providing a research leave under the auspices of the Faculty Academic Study Program, and I am especially grateful for the financial support extended by its President's Coordinating Council on International Programs. In the British capital, the London School of Economics served as a very comfortable base of operations for my year overseas as I was appointed a visiting research scholar. I am particularly thankful for the efforts of Dominic Lieven on my behalf. Research was also carried out in Amsterdam, where the Shipping Research Bureau (most notably Jaap Woldendorp) and the Holland Committee on Southern Africa were of great assistance.

The staffs of numerous libraries were instrumental in the research process, especially those at Rutgers University (including the Law Library), the School of Oriental and African Studies, the International Maritime Organization and the Marine Library. The British Library of Political and Economic Science at LSE not only provided numerous valuable materials, but also a comfortable private study room where most of this book was written. The publication *Lloyd's List* generously permitted access to its back issues.

Among those individuals who contributed significantly to the research were Martin Bailey, Stuart Bell, Robert Bishop, Barbara Conway, Gerald Cooper, Lee Coppack, Peter Fishbein, Peter Griggs, Brenda Gruss, John Masters, Kenneth Mayer, Clive Nelson, Theo Nijenhuis, Steven Schlesinger, Anastasios Tzamtzis, and Gillian Whitakker. Special thanks go to Eric

ACKNOWLEDGMENTS

Ellen, Director of the International Maritime Bureau, for his strong support and to Keith Pieterse, who provided translations from Dutch sources. Mohamed Ben-Madani must surely be cited for his sound advice regarding publication arrangements.

Of course, the views presented in this study are solely those of the author.

■ Prologue

■ Most of the perpetrators of the *Salem* fraud are known and
their motivation was, quite simply, greed. This story is therefore
not a whodunnit, or an analysis of why the crime was
committed, rather it is an examination of the conditions which
made such an act possible, and the means used step-by-step to
carry out successfully the biggest fraud in maritime history. The
system was outwitted, and the fascinating details of this process
provide the answer to the question: How was such a gigantic
fraud accomplished?

Frauds are based on game situations, intriguing challenges, in
which criminals seek to compromise the security controls of a
system. They may try to circumvent them, overwhelm them, or
corrupt them, but frauds will not succeed unless the system is
flawed and bears the seeds of its own subversion. Conditions
must be conducive, and they may even be seductive. In the
helter-skelter economic environment of the late 1970s, inflation
was rampant and oil, gold and diamond prices were soaring.
Currency was losing value, but commodity markets were
booming. Entrepreneurs were hustling to derive quick profits
before the chaotic financial tide shifted, while the security
controls of the international economic and legal structures were
straining to keep pace with rapidly evolving trends. Money,
people and documents were in frenetic motion on an unprecedented scale, and international boundaries were becoming
obfuscated by the growing globalmania. Paperwork lagged
behind transactions, and the law could not keep up with those
striving to evade it. The shipping and insurance industries were
in crisis, and the oil trade was rapidly attracting con men and
hucksters trying to take advantage of the spiralling prices and
the shortage of crude. In the *Salem* case, the imposition of oil

1

sanctions against South Africa also proved crucial as a commodities netherworld developed to maintain the supply. Some degree of economic chicanery was inevitable, but the *Salem* fraud proved to be more daring, complex and vast than anyone could have imagined.

Conditions may breed criminality, but only certain persons exposed to them opt for such a course. Personal responsibility must be the keynote, and the *Salem* perpetrators were no exception. Opportunity beckoned, and they seized the initiative. They acted on the basis of free will, with a quest to succeed but with a potential to fail. These fraudsters were surely not aspiring supermen with an inherent belief that they were unaccountable to the system and its laws, nor self-styled intellects, toying with mere mortals, who felt that inferiority merited its debilitating consequences. They were neither dashing heroes nor perfidious scoundrels but extremely ordinary people with hopes, fears and frailties, universal everymen who were attracted to the altar of Mammon.

The *Salem* case represents an ethical reversal, a perversion of an attempted good deed. Just as knights must occasionally give way to knaves, so an effort to impose perceived morality may unintentionally produce venality. An oil embargo was applied against South Africa as a means of deflecting the apartheid state from what many considered an abhorrent racist course. This rather noble approach then engendered its own contradiction as numerous traders sought to undermine the embargo for their own pecuniary, non-political ends. Some shady operators went so far as to victimize South Africa, as they took advantage of the secrecy which Pretoria had itself imposed on its counter-sanctions operations. Concealing the means of obtaining oil provided a cover for illegality, and it was with this anticipation of South Africa's discretionary silence that the *Salem* plot was developed.

High drama at sea

■ It was off the West African coast on January 17 1980, about 120 miles southwest of Dakar, Senegal. At 10:50 in the morning, a crewman on the BP tanker *British Trident* noticed a ship approximately eight miles away. It appeared to be in trouble. Eighteen minutes later, an SOS message was received by radio. It came not from the stricken vessel itself, but from one of two lifeboats which had already been lowered into the rather friendly sea. The report was that everyone had safely abandoned ship, but it took an additional twelve minutes after the radio contact had terminated for the lifeboats to come into view. Barely seven minutes later, at 11:36, crew members of the *British Trident* watched with astonishment as the supertanker *Salem* slid beneath the waves.[1] It was classified as a VLCC (very large crude carrier), a giant vessel of almost 214,000 deadweight tons which stretched out for nearly a fifth of a mile! At a latitude of 12° 38′N and a longitude of 18° 34′W, the *Salem* glided to the bottom of the Atlantic and came to rest 13,000 feet beneath the surface.

Within an hour, fourteen Greeks and ten Tunisians were helped aboard the *British Trident*. After their lifeboats were hauled on deck, Captain Robert Taylor headed his ship toward Dakar and it was almost midnight when the rescued seamen arrived in the Senegalese capital. During the voyage to shore, they had been able to wash, eat and relax and they had also related the tale of their tragedy. Their tanker was en route from Kuwait to Europe with a full load of crude oil and was just then on its way to Tenerife in the Canary Islands to secure some fuel, more commonly referred to as bunkers. At 3:55 a.m. on January 16 there was an explosion in the pump room which led to

3

flooding in the engine room. It was feared that additional explosions would follow so the ship was abandoned and all crew members were in lifeboats by 4:30. They then drifted through the day and night, witnessing more explosions and fires. The last explosion took place at 9 a.m. on January 17. It was a hazardous and terrifying experience, which only ended when they were helped aboard the *British Trident* thirty-two hours after lowering themselves into lifeboats.[2] The Greek master of the *Salem*. Dimitrios Georgoulis, vividly recounted his gripping hours hoping for rescue: 'The electrician complain of heart problems so I told him that, well, relaxing, be quiet, pray and nothing will happen to you because what can I do now? We were, I mean we was on the boat and no help for him and then later on we saw some sharks around the boat and all of them they was scared and afraid that they're going to die. So I told them, I says, just relax, nothing else. Then also I cannot say that I was not in panic. I was also in panic too.'[3]

Captain Taylor reported that two members of the *Salem's* crew needed medical attention and that 'all of the men seemed to be in quite bad shape, some showing it more than others.'[4] On the other hand, his radio officer commented: 'They were dressed casually, were clean and I was surprised to hear that they had spent over a day in lifeboats.' The chief engineer recalled: 'I thought at the time that the condition of the crew was particularly good considering the length of time the Captain of the *Salem* had said they were in the lifeboats. I also noted that their clothing was in very good condition, that no one was dirty or had any oil on them.' In addition, observations by those aboard the *British Trident* did not confirm the fires and explosions described by the *Salem's* crew, with Captain Taylor saying that 'at no time did I see any flames nor smoke coming from Salem nor did I hear any explosion from Salem.'[5]

Other factors also stirred the curiosity of the *British Trident's* crew. The *Salem* evacuees had managed to pack clothing and other belongings, and boarded the rescue vessel carrying suitcases and attache cases. They had also saved the ship's registration certificate and a copy of the bill of lading, but not the critical log. The chief mate had all of the passports. Crew members also seemed to have an unusually large amount of money and cigarettes. In the lifeboats, there were sandwiches, crackers, apples and pistachio nuts. The water tanks were full, although some evaporated milk had been consumed. There was also plenty of extra equipment taken from the ship, much of it valuable and not ordinarily found on lifeboats.[6]

Captain Taylor estimated the size of the *Salem's* oil slick as three miles by half a mile, but he noted that 'there was not a considerable amount of oil on the surface of the water' considering that the supertanker was supposed to have been fully laden.[7] Other anomalies were soon apparent. Had the *Salem* been filled with oil, the type of explosions described by the crew would not have been possible. The ship's location was also off the normal route for tankers; the *British Trident* was only at that location fortuitously as it was adjusting its course after being notified of a change in its destination. Furthermore, the *Salem* had taken thirty-eight days to travel from Kuwait to its fatal point in the Atlantic, at least ten days too many for a vessel of its cruising speed.[8]

The *British Trident* did not pick up an SOS signal until the lifeboats were already adrift, more than a day after the first explosion on the *Salem* was said to have taken place. By then, the *British Trident* was probably visible from the *Salem*. Why didn't the *Salem* radio for assistance before the ship was abandoned? Afterwards, the limited range of the transmitter in a lifeboat would have rendered efforts much less effective. Master Georgoulis claimed that calls for help were sent, but no ships received them although the *Salem's* radio had a daytime range of 1500 miles and a night-time range of 2000! Furthermore, the lifeboats had engines. Why weren't they used? Why did the survivors of the disaster remain near their vessel rather than head for the Senegalese coast? Also puzzling was the account given about lowering the lifeboats. Almost a complete stoppage of the ship's forward motion would have been needed to accomplish this task, requiring an hour. It had been claimed that abandoning the *Salem* had taken only half an hour.[9]

And thus the tale of the *Salem's* last voyage began to unravel, and the mystery of the sunken supertanker began to unfold. It is an account of a victim who served as an unwitting accomplice to his own defrauding, and then was reluctant to bear witness; of missing evidence as the stolen goods turned out to be unidentifiable and irretrievable; and of the main instrument of crime lying, beyond examination, at the bottom of the Atlantic. Despite these impediments, numerous investigations were undertaken on three continents in a case involving more than twenty countries. The shipping and insurance industries were thrown into turmoil as the integrity of the entire maritime trade, and of several governments, was at stake. The *Salem* case entered the *Guinness Book of World Records* and aptly came to be known as 'The Fraud of the Century.'[10]

The plot takes shape

■ Oil prices were rising rapidly, and the opportunity to make quick and sizeable profits as a commodities dealer was very alluring. One of those attracted was Frederick Soudan, suave, raven-haired, and golden-throated. A Lebanese born in 1943, he had moved to the United States in 1972 and had become a naturalized citizen. Soudan was an outgoing and personable insurance salesman with expensive tastes and a restricted budget. He had plied his trade in Texas; then, in July 1977, he had departed for a year and a half of insurance work in Jordan. Soudan witnessed the Middle Eastern oil boom and returned to Houston with a plan. On February 9 1979 the commodities brokerage firm American Polamax International was formally incorporated as Soudan teamed up with Dr Lewis Newman, an educational consultant and career counsellor whom he had met in 1978.[1] Typically, Soudan was able to work out an arrangement under which Newman provided almost all of the capital.

In the Netherlands, Anton Reidel also hoped to move into the oil trade. Born in 1926 and greying, he was a supplier of duty-free goods to ships in Rotterdam harbour, a broker who generally traded in cigarettes and liquor and who was suspected by many law enforcement officials of being a smuggler. Reidel established Beets Trading in Zug, Switzerland as his commodities firm, but he also came up with the idea some time later of cleaning up the Rotterdam red-light district by placing prostitutes on ships.[2] Reidel was shrewd, organized, calculating and always on the lookout for a good deal.

In Greece, the swarthy Nikolaos Mitakis operated as a shipping agent along the Piraeus waterfront. Gregarious, a chain-smoker, and comfortable in the hustle and bustle atmosphere of Greek shipping, he was streetwise but yet unsophisticated. In his early fifties, he operated two companies, Mitzinafir Navigation and the Euroafrican Corporation. Mitakis had developed a reputation as a man whose ships experienced an unusual number of casualties.[3] He first met Reidel in May 1979 and on June 14 Mitakis telexed him with the message: 'Please come to Athens, we have a very big deal for oil.'[4] The *Salem* escapade was underway.

Let's Make a Deal

Mitakis told Reidel that he could secure six 200,000-ton cargoes of Saudi crude to take to an embargoed destination like South Africa. Papers would have to be provided to show that the ship was presumably delivering oil to a refinery elsewhere. Panama was mentioned and the ship, after unloading in South Africa, would actually proceed to Panama to complete the charade. Mitakis also talked about the need for a bareboat charter.[5] Usually, the master and crew are provided by the shipper, or the company managing the vessel on behalf of the shipper. In a more costly bareboat charter, they are appointed by the charterer and he also has to furnish the provisions (food, supplies) and bunkers. In essence, Mitakis wanted to control the operations of a selected tanker by placing aboard his own master and crew.

Reidel was asked to find a buyer for the crude but, acting through middlemen, he failed to interest either Mobil or BP. He also tried unsuccessfully to approach South Africa directly. Another avenue of operation was collaboration with a West German named F.J. Dumee. On June 29, Dumee telexed the Dusseldorf office of the South African Coal, Oil and Gas Corporation (Sasol). At the time, it administered the Strategic Fuel Fund, which was used for procuring South Africa's oil imports. Dumee offered to supply oil, and he then sent more specific information to the SFF on July 2. Several communications were exchanged, including one on July 5 in which Dumee mentioned a bareboat charter and indicated that the shipping would be handled by the Euroafrican Corporation, registered in Panama and 'controlled by us.' It was Mitakis' company. No deal resulted, nor was any progress achieved when the oil was offered to the South Africans through Cape Town traders Danny Kahn and Laurie Goldberg.[6]

Meanwhile, Fred Soudan had teamed up with James Lovell, owner of the Dallas Fort Worth Oil Corporation, and they had travelled to Madrid where Soudan's knowledge of Spanish permitted him to assist Lovell as an interpreter. Lovell had hoped to purchase oil from some Nigerians, but he never got to meet them while in the Spanish capital. However, Lovell did meet with Reidel in both Amsterdam and Zurich, and he introduced Soudan to Reidel the last week of July. It was at this point that Soudan heard the details about Mitakis' proposal and be became interested in brokering the oil that Reidel said was available. Most likely, Soudan already had some notion that a large quantity of crude was being offered for sale as a European firm, Ecopetrol, had telexed Newman about it on July 18. Lovell was skeptical of the whole affair and returned to the United States, but Soudan persevered. He asked Sam Binion, a Louisiana oil worker with no experience as a broker, to help him work out a deal with Reidel. Binion knew Hans Von Lange, who managed the Intma trading firm in Baltimore, and he entered the negotiations too. Initially, Von Lange wanted to broker the sale of oil to Spain, but he then met with both Reidel and Mitakis to consider the proposal they were offering. Probably due to the participation of Soudan, the paper destination was to be Corpus Christi, Texas, rather than Panama, but the other details remained the same. Mitakis wanted his crew to board the anticipated tanker in Karachi, Pakistan, as a possible plan was to charter the *Marakanda* and take control there. Von Lange apparently was to look into the chartering of a ship but he became suspicious of the envisioned bareboat charter, the under the table deal with South Africa, the false documentation related to using Corpus Christi as a destination, and the intention to change the name of the tanker at sea before delivering to South Africa.[7] Von Lange pulled out of the negotiations, as did Irving (Chet) Perry of Illinois. Perry was president of ITEC Oil, and he was seeking crude to sell to Colombia. The oil Mitakis claimed to have available in Saudi Arabia interested him, but he had no intention of providing a ship that would be bareboat chartered to the Greek shipping agent.[8] Sam Binion also faded from the scene.

Reidel was having trouble working out an oil deal, so Mitakis opened up an alternative channel of communication with Henry

Donovan (Don) Seaton, an international trade consultant in New Orleans. Seaton had already been trying to arrange a delivery to South Africa via Bonaire in the Netherlands Antilles, but he needed a supply of oil. Mitakis did not at this stage inform Reidel about his contacts with Seaton as the latter was perhaps capable of finding both a buyer and a ship, rendering Reidel's role superfluous. Mitakis, maintaining that the oil had been stolen by a port captain in Ras Tanura, Saudi Arabia, told Seaton about the six cargoes he had available and the bareboat charter. He claimed that he had a nominal buyer who would verify receipt of the full load of oil even though the tanker would actually have only 10 percent remaining as the oil delivered to South Africa would have been replaced with seawater. Seaton and Mitakis kept in contact throughout September, and Seaton also dealt with Mitakis's associate Eleftherios Afentakis. In Athens on September 30, Seaton and Mitakis (Afentakis was also present) concluded an oil agreement, with South Africa being stipulated as the probable buyer.[9] Proceeding along several tracks, Mitakis, Reidel, Soudan and Seaton were attempting to put together an oil deal but, back in Houston, Soudan's partner Lewis Newman was becoming quite alarmed. He and his family had already invested at least $50,000 in American Polamax, but there had been absolutely no economic return. Newman did not believe that the negotiations with Reidel and Mitakis would be successful, and he felt that Soudan was moving into a financial netherworld that could lead their company into illegal transactions. Soudan dramatically responded to Newman's concerns: 'Doc, don't worry about Soudan. Soudan is like a shadow. They can see me, but when they reach for me, I'm not there.' Newman was not assured and he left American Polamax on October 2, 1979. The destitute Soudan then had to turn to John Haddad, Michael Kabalaki and his brother-in-law Abdul Wahab al-Ghazou as investors.[10]

First Piece of the Puzzle

Mitakis professed to have the oil, so securing a tanker was the top priority. As Mitakis did not have a good reputation in the shipping community, it was necessary to find a man with a clean record. He therefore turned to Fred Soudan. In the words of Peter Griggs, the Scotland Yard fraud squad detective who investigated the case: 'Well, it was that Reidel was to find somebody, and he found Soudan, who was the man up front, to buy the ship and do the necessary other things such as insuring it, and to sell to South Africa.'[11] Soudan knew nothing about shipping so he sought the advice of John Day, a British agent dabbling in both oil and shipping. In September, Day introduced him to a London broker named John Masters of the firm Elder, Smith, Goldsborough, Mort, Ltd.[12] Soudan asked Masters to find a tanker that could be bareboat chartered, and he indicated that his intention was to deliver oil to South Africa. Soudan maintained that a bareboat charter was needed to conceal the supposed involvement of Crown Prince Fahd of Saudi Arabia, with whom he was ostensibly acquainted![13] Masters stressed the difficulty of arranging a charter on that basis, especially for an oil run to South Africa.

Unwilling to rely solely on the efforts of Soudan, Mitakis was working with Seaton as well. The Louisiana trade consultant was therefore out searching for a bareboat charter, and he engaged the assistance of a British agent named Roger Conway Hyde. Hyde contacted London shipbrokers, including John Masters. Masters had already heard the same basic proposal from John Day, acting on behalf of Fred Soudan, and he realized that Day and Hyde were operating from different directions but trying to put together the identical deal. Masters stayed with Day and continued to serve as a broker for Soudan. Hyde had to turn elsewhere to serve his client, Don Seaton.[14]

While Soudan and Seaton were looking for a ship, Mitakis was putting together a crew in Piraeus. With him the first few days of October was a mysterious figure who called himself 'Bert Stein,' which was actually a name written into a blank passport that had been stolen in Frankfurt in 1976.[15] Mitakis later testified that 'Stein' had called him several times over a period of eighteen months, but that this was the first time they had ever engaged in business together. Reidel didn't meet 'Stein' until afterwards, when Mitakis introduced them.[16] 'Stein' and Mitakis selected a crew and appointed Dimitrios Georgoulis as master, his brother-in-law Andreas Annivas as chief officer, and Antonios Kalomiropoulos as chief engineer.[17]

Soudan perhaps unrealistically thought that he could get a tanker, but he had no customer for the oil. Seaton seemed to have better prospects in that area so Soudan contacted him the last week of September to offer help in providing a ship. Soudan and Seaton stayed in contact as there was some possibility that they could work together. At the same time, they pursued their separate searches for a bareboat charter. Although Soudan may have thought he had the inside track, it was actually Seaton who found a ship first and he arranged to have it inspected. Georgoulis and Kalomiropoulos went to Gibraltar about October 4 and took a trial run in the 214,000 ton Liberian-flag tanker *Paula* as it sailed to Malta. They found it to be a satisfactory vessel and Mitakis assembled his twenty-six officers and crewmen in Malta on October 11 to wait for boarding. No deal was reached in the negotiations on the ship, and they ended on October 20. The owners were willing to sell the vessel but, if they chartered it, they would not do so on a bareboat basis. In any case, no money was yet available to charter the *Paula*. Seaton had been attempting to secure financing but he had run into difficulties as he had no evidence that there was a cargo of crude to transport. Mitakis failed to provide the 'stem number,' which offers proof that a cargo is being placed at the disposal of a buyer, as the Greek shipping agent conversely asserted that he couldn't get a commitment on the oil until there was clear indication of a tanker to transport it![18] Nevertheless, Seaton and Reidel did not give up the idea of purchasing the *Paula* until early November. In the meantime, the prospective officers and crew members lounging in Malta were flown to Dar es Salaam, Tanzania (arriving there November 2) and told to await further instructions.

Oil for Sale

Fred Soudan needed connections in South Africa, and he eventually developed an association with John (Jack) Austin and James (Jim) Shorrock. Austin, a metals consultant, had communicated with Soudan in August or September about securing American financing for the exploitation of bayrite deposits in South Africa. Bayrite was a mineral used in drilling. No bayrite deal was worked out, but Austin had also asked if Soudan could supply oil, and he had answered affirmatively.

Operating along a second track, Soudan also got in touch with Shorrock. He was a salesman, allegedly involved in a marketing scandal, who had recently decided to try his hand as a commodities broker. A trader in Paris named Herbert Thoener (also spelled Turner in many documents) brought Soudan and Shorrock into contact, and it is possible that John Day was the link between Soudan and Thoener. Thoener informed Shorrock about October 7 that Soudan had oil available, and Shorrock's wife then called S.P. (Fanie) Naude, crude oil manager of the Strategic Fuel Fund.[19] Naude was interested, so Soudan telexed him on October 8 with an offer of six loads of crude. He mentioned the *Paula*, and said it would be operated by the Euroafrican Corporation, Mitakis' company. Naude telexed tentative approval the next day and, on October 12, he asked Soudan to visit him in Sasolburg for discussions on October 15 or 16. He indicated that Soudan was expected to pay his own expenses, but his finances were in such poor shape that he had to borrow money for the trip from his cousin Wahib Attar. In return, Attar received one-quarter ownership of American Polamax.[20] Austin and Shorrock then became Soudan's representatives in South Africa, registering their firm Haven International on October 19.

Soudan, an immigrant from Lebanon and an aspiring commodities broker, now had the opportunity of a lifetime. He had to make the most of the situation. At an October 15 meeting with Naude, Jan Bredenkamp and other SFF officials, he regaled his audience with tales about knowing many Arab political dignitaries, constructing a huge new corporate headquarters for American Polamax, owning the Goodhope refinery in Louisiana, and owning the Dallas Fort Worth Oil Corporation (actually owned by former colleague James Lovell). He claimed that he operated 255 drills and 140 wells, supplied Israel with oil, and had 37.5 million barrels of Saudi oil (more than five million tonnes!). His supposed refinery could only process 250,000 barrels per day so he had a surplus on his hands and wanted to sell it to South Africa. He certainly gave the impression of being a man of substance and the South Africans, desperate to secure oil from any source in the face of an embargo by all OPEC countries, did not bother to check out his claims. Soudan even offered to donate $500,000 to local hospitals!

Soudan (joined by Austin) and the South Africans discussed the dispatching of six cargoes of 200,000 tonnes each, to be

13

delivered at seventy-day intervals. The first cargo would be priced at $33.50 per barrel, and subsequent cargoes at $33. Soudan said that he would leave 10 percent of each tanker's cargo on board and would take it to his own refinery. Then he would certify that all the oil had been received in the United States. Corpus Christi, rather than South Africa, would be the official destination. In order to facilitate such paperwork, the original bill of lading would have to be provided in the US but he said that the South Africans would be presented with proof that he owned the oil. Naude was prepared to start with the purchase of one or two cargoes, but he would not accede to Soudan's request for payment in advance. Soudan indicated that he needed a ship as he didn't have his own available at that time due to a boiler problem. Naude had no interest in having South Africa purchase a ship to deliver the oil, but he was willing to consider the extension of a letter of credit to Soudan.[21]

Confusing the negotiations were the actions of Don Seaton. He was simultaneously Soudan's collaborator and rival, and he was offering oil to the SFF at a price lower than Soudan's. In fact, he had contacted Naude the previous day still intent on making a deal. SFF officials did not quite understand his relationship to Soudan so, on October 15, Jan Bredenkamp called Seaton to seek clarification. Seaton said that he had oil and that Soudan and Reidel were planning to buy it from him. He also said that he was expecting to buy the *Paula* and was willing to deal directly with the SFF. Soudan told Bredenkamp that Seaton had been 'suspended' and the South Africans, ignoring Seaton, continued their talks with Soudan.[22]

The following day (accompanied by Austin and Shorrock), Soudan and Naude signed an agreement for a 214,000 ton cargo of Saudi crude, plus or minus 10 percent, at $33 per barrel. Payment was to be made through Zug, Switzerland (the location of Reidel's company), contingent upon the presentation of various shipping documents. Ninety percent of it was to be disbursed immediately once the ship started discharging. The delivery date was fixed at February 5-10 1980 and it was stipulated that the buyer would be permitted to board in Karachi so as to supervise the loading and subsequent unloading of the vessel. Karachi was mentioned because, at that time, there was still the expectation of chartering the *Paula* and dispatching the crew from Malta to board it there. At the end of the October 16 meeting, Soudan was asked if he could possibly deliver the oil earlier than February. He said he would look into it. He then called on October 18 to say that he would supply a cargo in December, but he raised the price to $34.70 per barrel. The Houston broker maintained that this cargo was separate from the anticipated delivery in February, and he had to take rising spot market prices into account.[23] Fred Soudan therefore had the deal he had been hoping for, and the South Africans thought they had little to worry about as no money would be turned over until the oil was delivered. The SFF had also contracted for oil at a very favourable price, despite Soudan's unilateral increase.

Meanwhile, Don Seaton had found Rumania to be a willing buyer of his oil and he obtained a $43 million letter of credit to purchase it. This took place just before Soudan visited the SFF, but Mitakis preferred a deal with South Africa as it would provide greater secrecy for his plan. He therefore did not join with Seaton in the Rumanian transaction and waited to see the outcome of Soudan's endeavours. Interestingly, Nikolaos (Nick) Makris joined Mitakis and Seaton in the discussions about Rumania. He was a Greek shipper who had lived in Australia for several years, and he later was to face charges in the *Salem* case. Once Soudan was successful, Mitakis opted for him and the Rumanian deal fell through. Soudan now had an oil agreement. He thus had to get a tanker quickly as he was committed to a December delivery date.[24]

Squaring the Circle

Fanie Naude had left open the possibility that Soudan could obtain a letter of credit, to be used to buy a ship. However, Soudan did not immediately explore this avenue as he thought he could secure financing from a bank in New York. He then ran into difficulties as a performance bond on the provision of oil was required, but Don Seaton was unable to obtain funding for the bond. Once it was apparent that Seaton could not come up with the bond, Soudan turned to South Africa to seek a letter of credit. The Strategic Fuel Fund was willing to help, but it was not a bank and could only assist Soudan, not actually provide the credit. The Haven International brokers, Austin and

Shorrock, were eager to be of service but they were just getting started in this line of work and did not have established ties to the banking community. On November 20, they therefore brought in consultants from the Mon Repos group, Daniel Fourie and Johan van Vuuren, to help find a bank willing to extend a letter of credit to Fred Soudan. For his part, Soudan returned to South Africa to join the quest for funds.

The Nedbank seemed supportive, but it delayed any financing as it needed the approval of the South African Reserve Bank. Soudan was so confident of receiving its help that, on November 23, he sent a letter to the SFF authorizing it to reimburse Nedbank out of the oil delivery payment.[25] However, there was no need to place all of his eggs in one basket. Later that day, Fourie arranged for him to see Manie du Plessis, international division manager at Mercabank. Soudan explained that he had an oil deal with the SFF but he was short of cash as he had already paid for the oil. He also said that he couldn't use his own tanker as it would be blacklisted after delivering crude to South Africa. Du Plessis was amenable to financing Soudan (Mercabank did not require Reserve Bank approval), but he had some preconditions: assurances that Soudan owned the oil, that Mercabank would get paid off the top by the SFF once the oil was delivered, and that the hull insurance policy would be ceded to his bank. Once these assurances were provided, a letter of credit would be made payable when Soudan furnished the sale documents for a ship.[26]

Du Plessis contacted the SFF and Soudan's deal with that organization was confirmed. Of course, du Plessis did not know that the SFF had never investigated Soudan's claims, including his professed ownership of oil. Apparently, the SFF's verification of its agreement with Soudan was sufficient as du Plessis seems to have dropped his request that Soudan's ownership of the oil be substantiated. As for getting reimbursed by the SFF once the oil arrived, it was decided that the SFF would transfer $12.3 million from its account at the Volkskas Bank, this amount to be subtracted from the sum owed Soudan for the oil. Then Soudan agreed in writing to a cession of a lien on the oil, a cession of the hull insurance, and the registration of a lien on the ship. The liens were to cease once Mercabank received its reimbursement from the SFF. With all of these details taken care of, Mercabank extended a letter of credit to Fred Soudan for $12.3 million and he agreed to pay interest on this financing.[27]

Mercabank seemed to be protected in every way, but the problem was that the liens and cessions were not recorded by Soudan in Liberia as stipulated (Soudan was intending to purchase a tanker that would be registered in Liberia). Mercabank was therefore in an exposed position and Dr Dirk Mostert, director of the SFF, later said that it was unclear what would have been the repercussions on Mercabank had the ship sunk or failed to deliver the oil.[28] A report to the South African parliament, prepared by the SFF, was more specific about the SFF's obligation to reimburse Mercabank: 'No payment would have been made had the ship not delivered the oil or had it sunk en route to the RSA. It is, therefore, inexplicable why the merchant bank agreed to finance them. Two other banks had refused to extend credit to the buyers of the ship on these conditions.'[29] Unstated was the fact that the SFF had played an important role in helping to arrange financing for Soudan. In all fairness, however, the SFF had nothing to do with stipulating the terms under which the letter of credit was to be proffered. Fred Soudan surely received financing in South Africa, and that country unwittingly assisted a plot which eventually led to its own defrauding. On the other hand, South African officials are correct in maintaining that a private bank, not an agency of the South African government, provided money for Fred Soudan. It should also be added that Mercabank itself borrowed the money for the letter of credit from Manufacturers Hanover Trust, and later repaid it on December 31.[30]

Without laying out any of his own funds, Soudan was in a position to buy a ship. Mitakis apparently had the oil, and South Africa had contracted to be the buyer. Soudan had combined his charm and rhetorical skills with his ability to avoid letting debts catch up with him. In this case, he promised a $200,000 commission to the Mon Repos group, with half then being filtered off for Haven International. Half of the commission was payable on December 2, and the remainder by December 10. Van Vuuren and Fourie complained when they did not receive their money, and Soudan said it had already been sent.[31] As Soudan had explained to Dr Newman, he was indeed like a shadow that wasn't there when others reached for him.

Laying the groundwork

■ Before Mercabank had agreed to provide a letter of credit, Soudan had already been searching for a ship to bareboat charter. He had received assistance from the Northern Ships Agency in New York and he was using the services of the London firm Elder, Smith, Goldsborough, Mort Ltd. Now he was in a position to buy rather than charter and attention had come to be focused on the *South Sun*, a tanker of 213,928 deadweight tons and 96,227 gross tons.[1] It was built in Sweden in 1969, was originally owned by Salenrederierna of Stockholm, and was the pride of the Swedish tanker fleet under the name *Sea Sovereign*. In 1977, it was sold to Pimmerton Shipping Ltd of Monrovia, renamed the *South Sun*, and began to fly the Liberian flag. It was managed by Wallem Ship Management of Hong Kong and, ironically, chartered to its first owner Salenrederierna. The *South Sun* served as a carrier of crude oil and it was suspected of having made some deliveries to South Africa.[2]

Pimmerton was unwilling to bareboat charter the *South Sun* to Soudan as he was not known in shipping circles, but it was prepared to sell the tanker. Once Soudan was assured (on November 23) of financial backing from South Africa, he moved quickly to buy the *South Sun*. John Masters, working with Pimmerton's broker Houlder Brothers, arranged the sale on November 27 for $12.3 million. This included the cost of the ship, bunkers left on board, and commissions to be paid by Pimmerton out of the purchase price. Roughly, the commissions were broken down into $100,000 for Houlder Brothers; $70,000 for Elder, Smith, Goldsborough, Mort Ltd.; $7500 for John Day; and $20,000 as an 'address commission' (which could be interpreted as a form of discount) for Fred Soudan. Soudan therefore acquired a ship without putting up any of his own

18

money, and he even received a commission! The $12.3 million price happened to be identical to the value of Mercabank's letter of credit as the latter had obviously been geared toward the purchase of this particular ship at the stated price. The sales agreement stipulated that Soudan would take delivery of the vessel in Dubai and that Pimmerton would be paid in London by a letter of credit issued through the Manufacturers Hanover Trust Company. Anton Reidel was present at the closing as a representative of Soudan. It seems as if Mitakis wanted him to attend to make sure that there would be no repetition of the terminated *Paula* negotiations. Everything went smoothly. On November 30, Pimmerton received payment and the deal was completed.[3]

Fred Soudan did not bargain over the price of the *South Sun* (he had Mercabank's letter of credit for the full amount anyway). He also did not have the ship inspected by a surveyor, even though it had been in the Gulf awaiting sale since November 16. Soudan was in a hurry to fulfill his contract with South Africa and he could not be concerned with the finer points of ship purchasing. According to Masters, he didn't even seem to care who would operate his new tanker.[4] After endeavouring so hard to secure it, Fred Soudan never set eyes on his vessel.

John Masters introduced Soudan to the insurance brokers Lowndes Lambert and coverage was arranged within two days. Although Soudan had no track record as a shipowner, Masters was a respected shipbroker and the *South Sun* was in no way suspect. Consequently, Soudan was able to insure the tanker for $24 million for a period of one year. In New York, a broker had offered only an $18 million policy for a similar premium. Masters had acted correctly in his capacity as a broker, but he had become privy to some interesting information. Soudan told him that the ship would be used to deliver oil to South Africa, and that this visit would then be covered up by directing the *South Sun* to Corpus Christi, Texas. Soudan explained that he could not afford to have his ship blacklisted by Arab states due to its involvement in the South African oil trade. Masters accurately declared several years later: 'As there is nothing illegal in this, insofar as British law is concerned, I saw nothing wrong in associating my company with the purchase of the *South Sun*.'[5]

Soudan had been in contact with the Northern Ships Agency in New York since late October. At first, he hoped to secure financing to buy a tanker, but the Greek-American directors of the firm, John Avgerinos and Andrew Triandafilou, were not amenable and suggested that Soudan obtain a letter of credit. However, they agreed to sell him a shipping company to serve as the registered owner of his anticipated tanker. On November 23, when Soudan had been successful in his negotiations with Mercabank, he called Northern Ships and said that he was prepared to buy the Oxford Shipping Company from Avgerinos and Triandafilou. This was before Soudan had contracted to purchase the *South Sun* as he was apparently quite confident of his ability to get the ship. The directors of Northern Ships were prepared to sell Oxford, a Shell company incorporated in Liberia in May 1973 that did not own any ships or have other assets.[6]

On November 27, the day that he contracted to buy the *South Sun*, Soudan bought Oxford Shipping. In an agreement worked out by his New York lawyer Zuhayr Moghrabi, Soudan was to pay $300,000 on or about December 27 once the *South Sun* had arrived at Durban, South Africa. In case no delivery of oil was made to South Africa, Avgerinos and Triandafilou would receive only $25,000. Soudan was to get all five hundred shares of Oxford stock, these shares to be held in escrow by the lawyers for Northern Ships pending receipt of Soudan's payment. The sellers were to resign as officers and directors of Oxford. Then they promised to elect Soudan and his wife as directors, him as president, and her as secretary. Soudan agreed to cede $300,000 of his insurance on the *South Sun* to Northern Ships to protect against a casualty occurring prior to the planned oil delivery in Durban, which meant that promises had been made both to Mercabank and Northern Ships regarding the same hull insurance. Actually, Soudan never followed through with his cession to the New York shipping agents, as he had similarly failed to do with Mercabank. Soudan now had a shipping company under his control, although he didn't sign the contract of purchase until December 8 and Avgerinos and Triandafilou did not affix their signatures until December 10.[7] Note that the directors of Northern Ships clearly knew about Soudan's intent to supply South Africa with oil, as did John Masters.

Mitakis had always stressed the importance of a bareboat charter so that the movement of the ship could be controlled by his own crew. Soudan had been unable to arrange such a charter, but now he owned his own ship. Would permitting someone else to bareboat charter the *South Sun* make any sense? Apparently yes as it would help obscure Soudan's role as owner of the ship and absolve him of responsibility. The bareboat charterer could be blamed for any improprieties, not Fred Soudan and Oxford Shipping. In practical terms, the charterer directs the master of the vessel, and the owner of the ship may not even be informed as to its destination. A bareboat charterer was therefore needed who would collaborate with Mitakis, Reidel and Soudan, provide legal insulation against any future inquiries or investigations, and place the assembled crew on board. Such a role could conveniently be played by the elusive 'Bert Stein.'

Bareboating

Hasso Osterkamp was an air-show organizer and former Luftwaffe pilot, a man with no criminal convictions who was looking for a challenging opportunity. In 1979 in Frankfurt, he ran into 'Bert Stein,' whom he may have first met in Turkey four years earlier. 'Stein' said that he knew people in Switzerland who wanted to get involved in oil trading and asked if Osterkamp was interested in helping out. He answered affirmatively and then opened three firms, apparently with 'Stein's' money. In October, 'Stein' arrived in Zürich, paid Osterkamp for his assistance, and assumed operation of the companies. One of them had originally been controlled by Heinrich Frey, a dentist who allegedly had been convicted of fraud. Frey had turned it over to Osterkamp, who then transferred it to 'Stein.' In October, it was registered as Shipomex in both Zürich and Monrovia, Liberia. 'Stein' then opened a Shipomex office in Zürich, which was rented to him by Frey.[8]

The *South Sun* negotiations had dragged on longer than anticipated. At first, Soudan had to secure financing; then Pimmerton delayed signing until some amendments were made to the letter of credit. On November 25, before the vessel had been purchased, arrangements were already being made to bareboat charter it. Reidel and Wahib Attar, Soudan's lawyer, were at Heathrow Airport near London and Attar phoned Stuart Hyde of Houlder Brothers, the brokers for Pimmerton. He demanded that the sales contract for the *South Sun* be signed by

6 p.m. that day. It wasn't as Pimmerton was still awaiting clarifications regarding the letter of credit. Nevertheless, a bareboat charter agreement for fourteen months at a rate of $285,000 per month was worked out. It was dated one day ahead, apparently in the hope that the ship sale would be concluded by then. This Oxford-Shipomex agreement was signed by 'Bert Stein' and Wahib Attar, but it is uncertain if Attar actually met 'Stein' (Reidel indicated that 'Stein' signed and that the Dutchman then gave the document to Attar and Soudan). Attar, on behalf of Soudan, had also signed the agreement to purchase the *South Sun* from Pimmerton. On that occasion, Triandafilou had authorized him to sign for Oxford. The ship was to be delivered to Shipomex in Dubai on November 27-30 and charter payments were to be made to a bank in Zug, Switzerland, where Anton Reidel's Beets Trading also had an account.[9]

'Stein' was known to Mitakis, but there is no evidence that he ever met Soudan. When Soudan agreed to bareboat charter his tanker to Shipomex, he was therefore turning over operation of the *South Sun* to a stranger, but he must have gained some confidence from the fact that Mitakis had a major role in selecting the crew. South Africa's Strategic Fuel Fund and Mercabank were not informed of this bareboat charter arrangement for a vessel that had been financed through the latter's letter of credit.

Also on November 25, Soudan and Reidel agreed that the oil delivery to South Africa would take place between December 25 and January 4 and that Soudan would receive $4.5 million out of the Strategic Fuel Fund's first payment, to be deposited in an American Polamax account in Zug. The bareboat charter to Shipomex was also mentioned in this document. In an annex, it was stipulated that Beets Trading would transfer to Soudan $11,650,000 'after first discharging' to purchase the ship from him.[10] Soudan was thus to serve only as a front man until the oil reached South Africa; then Reidel would take over the tanker. John Masters was therefore correct in his earlier assessment that Soudan seemed to be serving as a broker for Reidel.[11]

All Aboard

The crew assembled by Mitakis and 'Stein' had been waiting in Dar es Salaam since the beginning of November. It was expected to board the *South Sun* there, but financial arrangements were not completed until after the ship had already reached the Gulf.[12] Finally, word arrived that the *South Sun* was being purchased and orders were given to fly to Dubai, where the tanker was resting at anchor after returning in ballast from Quintero, Chile. The chosen master of the vessel, Dimitrios Georgoulis, was told by Soudan on November 27 to take command on November 30, which accurately turned out to be the date when Pimmerton received payment. On the appointed day, he and his 24-man crew replaced the departing 42-man crew and Oxford Shipping applied to register the tanker in Liberia as the *Salem*, which officially became its name on December 3. Anton Reidel, as Soudan's representative, had been present in Dubai to inspect the ship's documents.

Chief engineer Antonios Kalomiropoulos and chief mate Andrea Annivas were qualified, experienced and licensed officers. Master of the *Salem* Georgoulis was another matter. The trim, bearded, 43-year-old seaman later admitted that he did not possess a master's license or any kind of Greek or Liberian license (he was a Greek national and the *Salem* was a Liberian-flag vessel). He did claim to have a Panamanian chief mate's license issued in 1966, but it was not produced for examination.[13] Georgoulis had served as master of smaller ships and had been at sea since 1956, with a two-year break living in the United States in 1969-71.

Georgoulis' name had been linked to three cases of cargo theft, the most notorious being that which took place on the *Alexandros K.*[14] This small Cypriot-flag vessel of just over 4000 deadweight tonnes was loaded with 3000 tonnes of steel bars at Bourgos, Bulgaria, in December 1978. It was expected to deliver them to Egypt but, mastered by Georgoulis, it was diverted to Piraeus. Greek authorities would not permit the ship to offload or leave so it remained idle until May 1979 when it changed its name to the *Leila* and stealthily departed. By then, its owner Gregorios Makrygiorgios had sold it to Georgoulis and a crewman named Samonas as part of an arrangement to cover a debt to them and avoid paying for necessary repairs. After selling its cargo in Lebanon, it was abandoned off that country's coast and it went aground. Georgoulis was suspected of complicity (although he was not aboard the vessel when sent adrift) and forbidden to leave Greece while the investigation was in progress. However, he managed to slip out of his homeland (although not on an American passport as some have claimed) to become the master of the *Salem*. One of the Tunisian crewmen on the *Alexandros K.* joined Georgoulis on his new command. Years later, Georgoulis was sentenced to four and a half years for his role in the *Alexandros K.* affair, but the appeals court reduced his term to four years in February 1987.[15]

Vassilios Evangelides, radio officer of the *Salem*, also had a colourful past. Serving in the same capacity aboard the *Brilliant* bound from Piraeus to Barcelona in August 1975, he failed to send out any distress signals from his floundering vessel until help was already near. Then, offers of assistance were turned down and the ship sank off Sicily, supposedly with its cargo of scrap copper aboard. The *Brilliant* was apparently owned by Gregorios Makrygiorgios, who also happened to have owned the *Alexandros K.*[16] Makrygiorgios was subsequently to be charged for his role in the *Salem* case.

Charter Redux

Mitakis, Reidel and Soudan had a ship and crew in Dubai and a contract to deliver oil to South Africa. One ingredient was strangely missing, the oil. Mitakis could not really have had sufficient stolen oil available as it would obviously have been loaded on the *Salem* and taken to Durban. It was also apparent that funds were not on hand to purchase the oil so another means of acquiring it had to be found. At this point, the *Salem* fraud went into high gear.

On November 27, Soudan had made agreements to buy both the tanker and Oxford Shipping. The same day, Mitakis began to seek a cargo as he informed George Ritsos of Genpe Shipping in Piraeus that the ship was available for charter. Mitakis could not really broker a deal by himself as his reputation was suspect, and such a large vessel would not usually be brokered in Greece. Ritsos was much more respectable and he had contacts in London. Mitakis had known him for several years, and he led Ritsos to believe that he represented Shipomex, the ostensible managers of the tanker. Mitakis hoped to charter the vessel to a company planning to load Saudi crude as Soudan's contract with the Strategic Fuel Fund stipulated delivery of oil from that country. He also had to make sure that the voyage route would permit diversion to South Africa. Mitakis therefore told Ritsos that any prospective charterer would be excluded from loading the ship in Iraq, Iran or Kuwait and that the intended voyage had to be westward.[17]

Shell needed a tanker in Kuwait at some time during the period December 1-10 so it could not abide by Mitakis' Kuwait exclusion. Reluctantly, that exclusion was dropped by Mitakis but Shell stopped considering the *South Sun* on November 28 as it was unable to secure information about the tanker's new owner and his purchase arrangement.[18] Ritsos then became party to serious negotiations with Pontoil, a firm based in Genoa, Italy, but which was operating through a subsidiary in Lausanne, Switzerland. Pontoil owned ships, but the one scheduled to pick up a cargo in Kuwait was being repaired. Pontoil therefore sought a tanker through its agent Nolarma, and this firm was then put in contact with Genpe via the services of the London broker Galbraith Wrightson. Pontoil wanted the option of sailing the ship to Japan, but it gave in on this issue as the Kuwait exclusion had been withdrawn. Apparently, Mitakis felt that he needed a charterer quickly and could not hold out for a Saudi cargo. Pontoil also agreed to the unusual request that only one grade of crude could be carried, as it planned to do so anyway. Most likely, Mitakis had insisted on this so that the South Africans could not possibly claim that a blended cargo violated their contract with Soudan. On November 29, a charter party agreement was worked out (by the brokers Nolarma and Galbraith Wrightson) between Pontoil and Oxford Shipping for one voyage.[19]

The charter party specified that Pontoil would deposit its fee in a nominated bank account to the credit of Shipomex, but Pontoil probably had no idea that Shipomex had already leased the ship under a bareboat charter. Soudan and Oxford Shipping had thus contracted for two conflicting charter parties, one for fourteen months and the other for one voyage only. If the Shipomex bareboat charter was legally valid, then the Pontoil voyage party was apparently not.[20] Pontoil could properly have sub-chartered the tanker from Shipomex, but it had actually chartered it directly from Oxford. Its oil would therefore be placed on a vessel controlled by Shipomex and its appointed master, Dimitrios Georgoulis. It is clear that Shipomex moved rapidly to collect the charter fee. On December 19, it asked Pontoil for nearly $1.8 million in freight charges. On January 11, it lowered its sights and demanded $400,000 for 'unexpected expenses,' primarily to cover anticipated bunkering costs. Its actions were quite unorthodox as brokers usually handled such requests. In addition, no final destination had been filed so transportation costs could not yet be computed. As will be explained, Pontoil did not forward any payments.[21]

Ménage à Trois

Soudan, Reidel and Mitakis were surging ahead with their plans, but Don Seaton had been left by the wayside. Seaton had lost out in his competition with Soudan to secure the South African contract, but he then continued to work with Soudan in the search for a tanker. Seaton believed that he could get the oil from Mitakis, and he hoped to load it on the vessel Soudan would buy and become the bareboat charterer as well. Mitakis had withdrawn his presumed oil supply from Seaton when Rumania was the intended purchaser, but Seaton thought that it was still available for delivery to South Africa. Therefore, Seaton had become Reidel's rival as both men sought to furnish the crude to fulfill Soudan's contract with the SFF. Mitakis had been the key to the *Salem* affair as he claimed to have the oil. Gradually, Soudan was moving to the forefront as he had arranged the oil deal with South Africa, and then the financing to purchase a tanker.

Seaton and Soudan had agreed that the former would supply the oil and bareboat charter a tanker. A contract was worked out for 190,000 tonnes of crude, and another one was written (but not signed) regarding a bareboat charter to Balkanian Shipping, which Seaton represented. The New Orleans trader obviously paid careful attention to details as he obtained a quote from Lowndes Lambert on insurance coverage for the contin-

26

gency that the *South Sun* would not be available for loading in the Gulf by midday, November 30. Soudan seemed prepared to collaborate with Seaton, but he insisted on a $500,000 performance bond on the provision of oil before he would permit him to bareboat charter his anticipated vessel. He then raised the required bond to $1,500,000 and Seaton was unable to secure financing. As of November 14, Soudan and Seaton were still exchanging communications about the performance bond, but it soon became evident that Seaton could not come up with the needed funds. On November 25, the Soudan-Seaton partnership formally ended as Attar cancelled the bareboat charter agreement on the ground that the necessary performance bond had not been furnished. Apparently, Attar did not like working with Seaton anyway.[22]

Reidel had been angered that Soudan was expecting to purchase oil from Seaton, so he tried to keep himself in the picture by directly contacting the SFF. On November 13, he had telexed Naude to claim that he was actually offering the crude through Soudan. He also discussed details of planned payment for the cargo, and mentioned that the *South Sun* would be bareboat chartered.[23] Reidel was surely overstepping himself, but Soudan quickly turned to him once Seaton had been shunted aside. Soudan had maintained contact with Reidel, and Attar had even asked him to put up a $500,000 performance bond to guarantee his provision of oil. By November 22, Soudan had decided to go with Reidel rather than Seaton and he told Jack Austin that Reidel would be supplying the crude for the SFF contract. Tellingly, Soudan's letter of credit agreement with Mercabank authorized the use of Reidel's signature on all documents.[24]

Soudan needed both oil and a bareboat charterer, and he had to act immediately if he was to fulfil his delivery contract with the South Africans. Reidel placed his presumed oil stock at Soudan's disposal, and no performance bond was requested. Apparently, Soudan had not even known prior to this time that Reidel and Seaton had been offering the same oil![25] The new Soudan-Reidel team sprang into action at once, and this explains why Reidel was so anxious to arrange the Shipomex bareboat charter agreement on November 25, just when the Seaton contract was cancelled. On November 27, Reidel was at the *South Sun*'s closing in London, and he was in Dubai on November 30 when Georgoulis and his crew boarded the tanker.

All the pieces were beginning to fall into place, but there was still one major problem: the contract with the SFF had specified Saudi crude, but the oil from Kuwait was to be pumped aboard by Pontoil. On November 29, as soon as the Pontoil deal was completed, Soudan told the South Africans that he would not be able to sail his ship into Ras Tanura, Saudi Arabia (that country's main oil terminal), due to heavy port congestion. Instead, he was going to load Kuwaiti oil presumably owned by Reidel. The quantity promised was slightly reduced as it had to conform to the amount Pontoil was planning to load. The South Africans, of course, had no idea that oil owned by Pontoil would be the *Salem's* cargo as they had been told earlier by Soudan that he owned the oil to be delivered. The SFF acceded to Soudan's change of plans, but lowered the price it would pay by twenty cents per barrel.[26]

The *Salem* then prepared to cruise from Dubai to Kuwait to pick up Pontoil's oil. Some Indian officers stayed aboard for the short voyage in order to familiarize the new crew with the vessel, and the *Salem* set off for the port of Mina al-Ahmadi with its own contingent of 25, plus two wives. Soudan's representative Wahib Attar greeted it upon its arrvial in Kuwait on December 5.[27] The fraud of the century was running smoothly as the perpetrators contemplated the loading of the *Salem* with millions of dollars of Pontoil's crude.

■ The payoff

■ To complete the next step of their scam, the *Salem* perpetrators still had to convert Pontoil's cargo into their own asset and to secure payment for it from South Africa. The process began on December 10 when Pontoil had 196,232 tonnes of crude pumped into the *Salem* at the port of Mina al-Ahmadi, Kuwait. A bill of lading indicating that this quantity of oil had been loaded was issued by the Ministry of Oil, and the certificate of origin and authenticity listed Italy as the destination.[1] Reidel immediately notified the South Africans that his Beets Trading Company owned the oil. The South Africans were therefore unaware that the cargo they were expecting aboard the *Salem* really belonged to Pontoil. That same day, the *Salem* departed from Kuwait with a crew of fourteen Greeks and ten Tunisians. Three of the crewmen who had boarded at Dubai had quit, and two seamen had since been added. The two women on the *Salem* presumably got off in Kuwait, but the wife of the electrician may actually have been aboard while the vessel cruised to Durban. After leaving the harbor at Mina al-Ahmadi, some crew members suddenly displayed an artistic bent. They painted out the S and A of the name SALEM displayed on the ship's side and then added an A at the end. The new moniker of the mysterious supertanker was thus the LEMA.[2]

Quick Profit

Georgoulis and his crew were planning to divert Pontoil's oil to South Africa, but they ended up stealing Shell's oil instead! As soon as the *Salem* had pulled out to sea, Pontoil contacted Shell to see if it was interested in buying its cargo of crude. On two previous occasions that year, Shell had made such purchases from Pontoil. In fact, 200,000 tonnes of crude aboard the *Paula* had been sold to Shell in July. Shell was apparently expecting to buy a Pontoil cargo later in December, but it was attracted by Pontoil's offer of an earlier cargo as it would be charged one dollar per barrel less. It was also given forty days to pay, rather than the more typical thirty. Shell, operating through its British affiliate Shell International Petroleum Company Ltd (which was carrying out the transaction as the Shell International Trading Company), was 'crude-short' at the time and therefore made an agreement with Pontoil on December 14. Shell was at first a little confused when it checked on the ship carrying the oil. Looking into the background of the *Salem*, it found out that there was indeed a vessel with that name but it was only slightly more than 7000 deadweight tonnes, hardly a super-tanker capable of transporting such a large cargo. The *Salem* was registered in Saudi Arabia and was a carrier of ore, oil and chemicals. Obviously the wrong ship, but then Shell ascertained that the *South Sun* had just been renamed the *Salem*; Shell also solicited information from the Lloyd's Intelligence Service, which tracks the movement of vessels, and all seemed to be in order.[3] On the face of it everything was, as Pontoil's cargo had been picked up as scheduled in Kuwait and the tanker was indeed sailing in the direction of Italy. Shell could not have known the intentions of Georgoulis, nor the fact that LEMA was curiously painted on the vessel's side.

Pontoil had a long-term contract with the Kuwait Oil Company for 450,000 tonnes per month so it managed to receive a very low price during a period when the cost of oil skyrocketed by the greatest amount in history. In addition, this particular cargo may have been one of the last of the loads to be lifted so its price per barrel was extremely favourable. Shell was buying at a volatile spot market price not cushioned by the effects of a long-term contract, so it had to pay dearly for the cargo. Under these circumstances, Pontoil probably made a profit of at least $13 million on a tanker-load of crude that it had owned for only four days and then sold to Shell for more than $56 million. Comparing the prices paid for the oil by Pontoil and Shell is rather difficult as Pontoil purchased it 'fob' (free on board), which meant that it paid only for the oil; its pumping into the tanker was gratis. Shell paid 'cif' (cost insurance freight), which included insurance and transport charges, and its purchase price also covered a bank's commission.[4] Pontoil may have paid as little as $26.50 per barrel, while Shell paid about $38. South Africa, which was generally paying the highest oil prices in the world due to its embargoed status and the premium it provided as an incentive to sellers, ended up paying $33.61 per barrel 'fob' for the same oil, or a sum of $34.50 once freight, insurance and evaporation loss were calculated into the price.[5] Shell therefore paid more than South Africa, but it must be realized that the SFF had received a very low price from Soudan. That was a main attraction of his offer, and he could well afford to undercut the market as he wasn't going to purchase the oil anyway.

Some suspicion has been cast on Shell's role as it is wondered why Shell paid such a lofty sum per barrel for the oil. Did Shell know that the tanker was headed for South Africa, where Shell could command a hefty price and also help supply its own refinery operations? At their trials, Mitakis and Reidel claimed that Shell must have known the true destination of the *Salem*, but no evidence has ever been provided implicating Shell. The oil giant could possibly have figured out the *Salem*'s intended route from clues available at the time Shell itself considered chartering the vessel. Remember that the *Salem*'s broker had insisted that the voyage go westward, and an effort strangely seemed to have been made to assure that a Saudi cargo would be placed aboard. However, investigations in the United States, Britain, Greece and the Netherlands all cleared Shell, and the apparently exorbitant price per barrel paid was not unusual given prevailing spot market conditions. Shell did not pay too much; Pontoil and the Strategic Fuel Fund paid very little.

Pontoil had purchased the oil cheaply, so it could have sold it on favourable terms no matter where the tanker was headed. More important is the issue of whether there was any collusion prior to the Shell transfer between the *Salem* perpetrators and Pontoil. The Pontoil-Oxford charter party includes a 'special provision' that may possibly imply that the oil was intended to go to South Africa. It states: 'Should Bill of Lading not arrive at discharge port on time then owners to release the entire cargo without presentation of the original Bill of Lading. Charterers hereby indemnify owners against all consequences of discharging cargo without presentation of original Bill of Lading.'[6] It is also interesting that Soudan always seemed confident that someone would charter his vessel by November 30, even though he was unknown in the shipping trade and he started offering the *Salem* before he officially owned it. Many tankers were available for charter at that time, so did Soudan already know that Pontoil would place its cargo aboard the *Salem*? A South African report is highly suspicious of the Pontoil arrangement with Soudan, and its presentation is buttressed by Mitakis' allegation that 'Stein has connections with Pontoil.' It is also argued that Pontoil would not charter a tanker from someone like Soudan unless it had an understanding with Shipomex, and that Pontoil paid more for the charter than the amount previously requested of Shell or later charged to Shell by Pontoil itself.[7] This South African analysis provides some interesting areas of inquiry, but the sticking point is that the *Salem* was indeed first offered to Shell. This action makes no sense if some secret arrangements had already been worked out with Pontoil. In addition, it is clear that the original aim was to ship Saudi oil. The charter with Pontoil for the lifting of Kuwaiti crude therefore represented a change in plans.

Pontoil had insured the oil aboard for $56.3 million, which was considerably more than its value upon loading in Kuwait but not an unreasonable sum, as Pontoil had to protect itself against a rise in the spot oil price while the tanker was at sea. This policy was transferred to Shell, but another policy worth an additional $5 million was also purchased as Shell had paid more for the oil than Pontoil and sought additional coverage. Pontoil's policy indicated that the shipment was en route to Italy, but it stipulated 'other voyages held covered.'[8] This was beneficial to Shell as it planned to deliver the oil to France and was considering the port of Le Havre. Georgoulis was ordered to sail toward Gibraltar. In order to account for the extra time that would be needed to divert the vessel to Durban and offload, he cleverly informed Shell that the *Salem* had boiler problems and would not be able to cruise as rapidly as previously anticipated.

The Delivery

Reidel and Soudan had become partners in dealing with the SFF but tension existed between them over the negotiations. Reidel felt that the oil to be delivered was his, so he should take the leading role. Soudan had worked out the delivery contract with the South Africans so he wanted to protect his position and make sure that Reidel could not cut him out of the deal. Since the SFF was informed that Beets Trading owned the oil, payment would be made to that organization. Soudan had led Naude to believe that he was a representative of Beets as well as American Polamax, and his telex of December 7 refers to Beets as 'our company.' On December 10, Reidel telexed the SFF that Beets owned the cargo, it would transfer title, and payment should go to the Beets account in a Zug bank. These instructions were not inconsistent with Soudan's arrangements but the Houston broker resented Reidel's effort to negotiate directly with the South Africans. Reidel's telex comment that Beets was 'the only authorized party to sell' seemed like a slap at him so he notified Bredenkamp that same day that Reidel's telex should be discounted as 'our subsidiary the local manager acted without direct approval.'[9] Nevertheless, Reidel and Soudan maintained their working relationship.

As the *Salem* proceeded toward Durban with Shell's cargo of crude, Reidel and Soudan were on their way to South Africa to complete the paperwork required to finalize the sale. Reidel had a cast on his recently injured leg so he brought along his son to assist him. Especially crucial was the bill of lading, which is acceptable as a transferable legal document indicating evidence of title to specific goods. A bill of lading had been issued when the tanker was loaded in Kuwait. When Reidel and Soudan (accompanied by Shorrock, Austin, Attar and Reidel's son) met with Fanie Naude and other SFF officials at Sasolburg on December 19, Reidel presented a bill of lading with Pontoil's name scratched out as consignee of the cargo. Reidel later claimed that he was actually serving as a middle man. Altering the document was thus necessary to protect the identity of the oil's owner as companies were reluctant to be linked publicly with undermining the embargo against South Africa. Reidel said that this was a general practice in dealing with South Africa and that the SFF had even requested that Beets Trading be used as a go-between in order to conceal the true owner. Reidel also asserted that he had presented the original bill of lading, which had been given to him by Mitakis. The Greek shipping agent denied that he had ever possessed the document and maintained that Reidel did not receive it from him. In fact, Reidel could not possibly have shown the original bill of lading.

It is conceivable that he thought his document was the original, but the actual bill of lading was mailed to Pontoil and subsequently forwarded to Shell. It displays no evidence of tampering. In all probability, Reidel had brought the master's copy of the bill of lading to South Africa. Bredenkamp and Naude claim that they did not see the original bill of lading, and Naude's notes of the meeting refer to 'the Master's non-negotiable copy.' Evidence seems to indicate that it was even stamped 'Master's copy' and 'copy nonnegotiable.'[10]

Using the bill of lading as proof of title to the oil, Reidel then joined with Soudan in signing a document stating that Reidel, through Beets Trading, was the 'sole owner and title holder' of the oil aboard the *Lema* (note that *Lema* rather than *Salem* was cited). They also attested: 'In view of your agreement to pay for the above crude oil without the transfer of the negotiable bills of lading to your Company, we, the undersigned, hereby jointly and severally hold you harmless and indemnify you against all claims which may be made against you by whosoever as a result of the bills of lading for this cargo not being presented to you.' It is therefore unambiguous that the bill of lading was not turned over to the SFF (although copies of the master's copy were) and that this indemnity was demanded as a kind of collateral by the South Africans. In addition, this declaration that Reidel owned the oil served to exempt the SFF from any claim that it may have received stolen oil. The South Africans had to be protected, especially as Reidel had asked Bredenkamp to make sure that port officials did not ask for the bill of lading nor look into the tanker's name on documents.[11]

In this same written statement, the final price of $34.50 per barrel is stipulated. Reidel and Soudan had managed to raise it, as an earlier contract had mentioned $33 and the shift from Saudi to Kuwaiti crude had dropped the price another twenty cents. The increased price had been accepted by the SFF earlier as Soudan had argued that the December delivery was distinct from the February delivery for which he had contracted, and a higher rate per barrel was mandated by spot market conditions. The total sum to be paid by the SFF was to be $48,300,000, of which 90 per cent was payable when the pumping system was connected to the tanker and the remaining 10 percent within forty-eight hours. Mercabank was to receive $12,361,500 off the top to cover its letter of credit and interest charges, while Beets Trading was to garner $31,108,500 through its account in Zug,

Switzerland.[12] There is an amazing discrepancy here of approximately $5 million, which will be discussed in a moment.

If they did not know earlier, Reidel and Soudan by now should surely have realized that the oil must have been stolen. Reidel certainly didn't own it, and he must have noticed, before defacing it, that the bill of lading cited Pontoil. What knowledge did the SFF possess? It could have been taken in by Reidel's account of protecting the real owner's identity, but it is difficult to determine whether there was omission or commission. The South Africans were used to unusual practices in the oil trade as they attempted to acquire cargoes by nearly any means possible in the face of an embargo by OPEC states. Falsified paperwork had almost become the norm. It was needed to circumvent the sanctions, so the SFF could not be very fussy about documents proffered. In this particular case, South Africa's Mercabank had already provided over $12 million so the deal had to be concluded without too much scrutiny.[13] On the other hand, SFF officials could have been more diligent had they desired. According to their contract with Soudan, they were permitted to place someone on board to supervise the loading of the vessel. Had this actually taken place, the SFF would surely have known that the oil belonged to Pontoil but Naude had informed Reidel as early as November 14 that no SFF representatives would board before Durban.[14] Furthermore, the SFF had failed to ascertain that the oil had been resold while at sea (perhaps Reidel and Soudan were also in the dark), and ignorance of this fact turned out to be extremely crucial and legally detrimental.

The *Salem*, disguised as the *Lema*, cruised southward. In a manner common to many tankers plying the South African trade, its name had been altered in an effort to avoid any blacklisting or retaliation after its visit. Such deception also served the interests of South Africa as it complicated efforts by opponents of apartheid to monitor its oil trade. Not unusually, all of the radio communications from the *Lema* had the same call letters that had been assigned to the *Salem*.[15] Port authorities in Durban had been aware for several weeks that the ship would be arriving as the *Lema*, and it was welcomed there on December 27. The next day, it officially discharged 180,392 tonnes of crude at the single buoy mooring situated one and a half miles offshore. A hydraulic problem with the pumping system was cited by Shorrock and SFF's director, Dr Dirk Mostert, as the reason why almost 16,000 tonnes remained aboard. In fact, delays in pumping forced the *Salem* perpetrators to pay some extra port charges for lapsed time, plus a fine for discharging less than the amount listed for off-loading.[16] However, some mystery remains on this score.

The December 19 indemnity statement signed by Reidel and Soudan indicates that the SFF was to pay over $48 million for the oil, while it in fact paid just over $45 million as 16,000 tonnes remained on board. This appears logical until one considers that the December 19 document mentioned that Beets Trading expected just over $31 million as payment, ostensibly after delivering the total cargo. Even after the SFF had reimbursed Mercabank the specified amount and had deducted various expenses, Beets Trading still emerged with over $32 million despite part of the cargo remaining on the vessel. It therefore appears that Reidel, Soudan and the SFF knew as of December 19, eight days before discharging, that some oil would remain aboard. This helps explain why the $31 million figure was too low and there was a discrepancy of about $5 million in the original arithmetic. There may not have been any critical pumping problem at all, just the retention on the *Salem* of oil which would be needed to complete a documentary fraud. Soudan had planned from the very beginning to leave approximately 10 percent of the crude aboard, to deliver it to Corpus Christi, and there receive certification that a full load had actually arrived in Texas. The convoluted accounting procedures in South Africa may have been part of this process. Interestingly, officials operating the single buoy mooring banned the *Salem* from making future discharges there. Many technical reasons were cited but there is no mention that a pumping problem prevented full discharge. Also, testimony by Jack Austin indicates his awareness of pumping problems causing a slow discharge, but he does not refer to any incomplete discharge. To further complicate the matter, Reidel claimed that the South Africans had recorded at least 70,000 barrels less than was actually discharged, depriving him of $2.5 million.[17]

The *Salem*'s visit to Durban was kept secret from Pontoil and Shell and an effort was made to hide it from the maritime community at large by having the tanker masquerade as the *Lema*. It was therefore important to secure the complicity of the crew. Money would go far in buying their silence. Returning to the ship from Durban on December 31, Georgoulis was accompanied by Panagiotis Daglas, a former boxer who had checked into the Royal Hotel the day of the *Salem*'s arrival. Daglas had cash to distribute, but he had not brought it with him from Greece. Once Georgoulis had phoned Reidel to say that the crew demanded payment, the money was forwarded to Johannesburg and a courier from Durban then flew there to pick it up. Tunisian members of the crew each received $300 in Swiss francs, but there were negotiations over the size of the payment to be provided after leaving the ship. The sum of $5000 per Tunisian was raised to $7500, and then the figure of $10,000 was agreed upon. The Greeks on the *Salem* were each rewarded with $1800 sent directly to their families back home, but the additional amount promised them is still a mystery.[18] Chief engineer Kalomiropoulos later admitted: 'We were promised money for breaking the embargo.' Reportedly, chief mate Annivas refused to ballast the vessel or fill the cargo tanks with seawater until his wife informed him that his funds had arrived. The ship therefore sailed in that condition for at least a day after departure from Durban.[19]

The *Salem*'s oil had been discharged at a buoy operated by Shell and BP, although owned jointly as well with Mobil and the South African fuel organization, Sasol. Is it therefore possible that Shell didn't know its oil had actually arrived in Durban? Shell could surely have been more alert, but there is no reason to believe it intentionally covered up the delivery. If it had known that its cargo was in South Africa, one can safely assume that Shell would have requested payment, which it failed to do until much later. Shell's lack of knowledge was somewhat understandable. The *Salem* was thought to be cruising toward France, and there was little reason to expect that the *Lema* was indeed the *Salem* (although the identical size of their cargoes should have raised eyebrows). Shell's contacts with the *Salem* were also extremely indirect. Communications from the ship were routed through Mitakis, Genpe, Galbraith, Nolarma and Pontoil before they reached Shell. Furthermore, the name *Lema* could easily have been mistaken for those of two other tankers of comparable size which were interestingly owned by Shell. The *Lima* reportedly had left the Gulf just before the *Salem*, and it passed Durban earlier that week on its way to the Netherlands. The *Limatula*, arriving from Brunei, actually docked in Durban about the same time as the *Lema*.[20]

Was the name *Lema* intentionally chosen in order to sow confusion? Motivation is difficult to prove, but this episode does not appear to be accidental. It would not be unreasonable to assume that the name was selected particularly as a result of its similarity to those of other tankers expected in the area simultaneously. After all, the aim was to conceal the ship's visit. However, some good research was required as the name *Lema* was selected at least as early as November 29.[21] One may wonder even further if the name *Salem* was picked with the same end in mind. It could easily be changed to *Lema*. In addition, the *Salem* could be (and indeed was) confused with another vessel of the same name. Such deception may have been part of the broader plan.

The Split

The *Salem* fraudsters hoped to reap millions of dollars from their venture, and they were not disappointed. Reidel, Mitakis and Soudan waited together in Switzerland for their big payday, and it came according to schedule on December 28. As soon as the oil started to be discharged in Durban, the Strategic Fuel Fund promptly began to disburse the funds due as payment for the cargo. Beets Trading received $31,108,500 that day and additional funds were sent on January 3 and 10, bringing the total to $32,172,644.[22] Quite a haul for stolen crude!

Following the money trail is extremely important if one wants to penetrate to the essence of a fraud, and it proved crucial to subsequent investigations and prosecutions.[23] The SFF paid over $45 million for the oil. A small amount was deducted as an interest charge, while almost $13 million was sent to Mercabank to cover the letter of credit for purchasing the *Salem*, interest, and other expenses such as bank fees, commissions for Haven International and Mon Repos middlemen and Thoener, and the ship's expenses in port. This left more than $32 million for the perpetrators.

Reidel served as the disburser of funds as he was the paper 'owner' of the oil and the SFF had agreed to furnish the payment to his firm, Beets Trading. As will soon become clear, Reidel had $7.92 million left after giving large sums to Mitakis and Soudan. Of that amount, he seems to have kept $4.2 million; $100,000 was dispatched to Spain, possibly to pay someone helping to arrange additional deliveries (although the account was in Reidel's name); and just over $2 million went to an account in Lugano, Switzerland. This leaves more than one and a half million dollars unaccounted for, and it is generally believed that such a payment must have gone to 'Bert Stein.' In fact, Reidel later claimed that 'Stein' received $1,620,000 in cash. On December 28, 'Stein' paid for his Shipomex office rental in cash and closed it. He also terminated the lease on his Zürich flat.[24]

The funds sent to Lugano appear to have been for Georgoulis and his crew.[25] Greek ship personnel had also received extra payments for the Durban diversion of the *Salem*, and they may even have shared in the funds that were given to Mitakis. Some therefore fared very well financially, and at least two immediately opened restaurants. It is even claimed that one person, bankrupt before the voyage, had $1.2 million in his account early in 1980. Georgoulis later indicated that the crewmen were paid yet another time prior to the Greek trial of 1985.[26] Silence was indeed golden!

Considering the share of the bounty retained by Reidel, it is obvious that he played an important role in the *Salem* fraud, but it is most unlikely that he was the mastermind of the plot, as later claimed by Dutch authorities. Most of the proceeds went to Greece and it is in that direction that we must look for some clues about the origin of the whole affair. Of the initial $31 million transferred by the SFF to Reidel, $20 million was on December 29 placed at the disposal of a gentleman named 'Nicholas Trilizas.' 'Trilizas' deposited the full amount in a Geneva bank and then withdrew all of the funds in three installments by January 10. The US Federal Bureau of Investigation identified 'Trilizas's' fingerprints as belonging to Mitakis, and the bank employee handling the account also identified Mitakis. At his appeals trial in 1986, Mitakis admitted that he had received $20 million using the false name of 'Nicholas Trilizas' and maintained that Reidel had given him a Greek passport for 'Trilizas' issued in Sweden.[27]

How much of this huge sum was kept by Mitakis remains a mystery. Nevertheless, there is no reason to assume that his role was worth so much more than those of Reidel and Soudan. It thus seems likely that most of the $20 million was given to others. Interviewed in 1980, Mitakis was asked: 'How much money did you make out of the *Salem*?' He responded: 'Money?

Huh. Well, what I have, I'll tell you. I got not any penny and that's it.' Six years later, he admitted pocketing $385,000 in brokerage fees and a commission per barrel of oil. He may have grossly understated his windfall as it was alleged at the Greek trials that Mitakis and fellow defendants Gregorios Makrygiorgios and Nikolaos Makris each received $6.5 million.[28] Of course, expenses must be taken into account, as associates and crewmen were given some of this money, and a portion must have been needed to cover the cost of extensive travel by the participants and maintaining a potential crew in Malta and Tanzania.

Anton Reidel said that Mitakis appeared to be subordinate to other Greeks. He cited meetings at which Mitakis seemed deferential in their presence, and he claimed that Mitakis gave two Greek associates about $1.5 million in cash after he had been paid as 'Trilizas.'[29] A BBC documentary aired in August 1980 charged that four Greek shipowners (this group did not include Mitakis) met at a restaurant near Athens to plan the *Salem* fraud, each contributing at least $250,000 to finance the operation. Their names could not be broadcast due to British libel laws, but it was alleged that one member of this quartet had received at least $2 million of the *Salem* proceeds.[30] As we shall see later, four Greeks were indicted for their involvement.

Anton Reidel declared that $2 million of the $4.2 million he retained had been owed to him for ten years by three Greeks associated with Makrygiorgios. He indicated that he insisted on handling the disbursement of the *Salem* funds to make sure he got paid, as he had failed to receive money due in the past from the same Greeks.[31] These revelations made at Reidel's trial passed with nary a yawn, but actually contained the nucleus of a bombshell. They implied that some Greeks conspired with Reidel to perpetrate the *Salem* fraud, and that one of the motivations was to secure sufficient funds to repay Reidel for an old debt.

Since Soudan owned the *Salem*, he was supposed to receive $4.5 million for a bareboat charter, minus $260,000 which represented half of the ship's expenses. A computation of the charter for fourteen months adds up to only $3,990,000, but it doesn't negate the basic proposition that Soudan's share of the proceeds was based primarily on shipping services rendered (especially if interest is factored in). Out of the original payment received by Reidel, Soudan was immediately given $3 million, and he got an additional $1.25 million in February 1980. Keep in mind that he also owned the *Salem*, which was worth more than $11 million and insured for $24 million.

Out of his $4.25 million, Soudan disbursed slightly over $2 million to pay Northern Ships, John Day, members of Haven International and Mon Repos, employees of American Polamax, lawyers, and the insurance broker Lowndes Lambert. Soudan therefore took care of all his obligations, albeit somewhat tardily, and he still had $2 million left despite Shell's success in freezing an account containing $120,000.[32] He told his friend John Haddad that he could explain his new wealth by claiming it was an inheritance from his father, who had died that December.[33] Fred Soudan was most generous toward his friends, relatives and colleagues, and he also began to live lavishly. He bought a new house for $298,000 in cash, a Cadillac, and probably a gold and platinum chess set worth several hundred thousand dollars. He also opened a Mercedes Benz dealership. He was living the good life in Houston, boom capital of the oil explosion, and he had funds tucked away in Switzerland, Luxembourg, Lebanon and the Bahamas. After exerting great effort, Fred Soudan had made it big. He was riding the crest of the wave, oblivious to the impending undertow.

Reidel, Mitakis and Soudan had successfully pulled off their fraud, but telltale clues had been left behind in South Africa which would soon reveal the secret visit of the *Salem*. Furthermore, the *Salem* had not yet finished its journey and considerable adventure still lay ahead.

■ Dénouement

■ The money realized from the *Salem* fraud was eagerly being stashed away, but complications soon developed which made the overall plan go awry. A bungled scuttling, insurance problems, and dissension among the perpetrators combined to take much of the lustre off the initial success of the cargo fraud. Millions of dollars in profits had been reaped, but much remained to be sown.

On January 2 1980, the *Lema* left Durban with 16,000 tonnes of crude still aboard. Some seawater soon had to be added as ballast, but a much greater quantity was in fact pumped into the tanks in order to make the vessel appear fully laden. The secret delivery to South Africa could thus be covered up, and the ship could cruise onward as if it still carried its entire cargo of crude. After moving out to sea, another paint job was accomplished as the *Lema* again became the *Salem*. By this time, Shell was very concerned about the location of the tanker, but Georgoulis reported that the boilers had been fixed and the *Salem* was proceeding on course.[1]

South African oil officials, and perhaps Fred Soudan, believed that the ship was headed for Corpus Christi, but such was not the case. It turned almost due north until it reached one of the deepest troughs in the Atlantic and, for reasons to be explained later, was then scuttled by flooding on January 16-17. The scuttling plan was set in motion in Durban as crew members were informed, and their complicity bought. The Tunisians were particularly upset that most of their belongings would be lost with the ship. As stores were taken aboard for the voyage ahead, it was evident that they were not sufficient to last until Europe and the word was spread that the scuttling would take place about January 14 or 15 near Dakar, Tenerife or Las Palmas.

After leaving South Africa, the seamen were given lifeboat assignments and instructions in putting on lifejackets. The lifeboats were also stocked with cigarettes and liquor.[2]

To prepare for the scuttling, petrol was spread and Kalomiropoulos and Papaleon allegedly removed some of the tanker's crucial metal plates. Approximately fifty sandwiches were also made for each lifeboat. At one point, another vessel came near so all of the *Salem*'s lights were turned off. Somewhat after 4 a.m. on January 16, the crew set off in lifeboats, but they never ventured more than three hundred metres from the ship. The propeller on a lifeboat was not operative so one lifeboat constantly held the other in tow. Smoke billowed from the *Salem*, but it had stopped before the *British Trident* came upon the scene. There were no explosions. Once the BP tanker was sighted, most of the cigarettes and liquor were thrown into the sea.[3]

The *British Trident* immediately reported the loss of the *Salem*, and Georgoulis used that ship's facilities to notify Shipomex in Zurich. Only an hour after the sinking, the insurance broker Lowndes Lambert was already notifying Fred Soudan by telex. The London shipping daily *Lloyd's List* included the *Salem* in its Janaury 19 casualty report, and the *Lloyd's Register of Shipping Casualty Return* reported the *Salem* as 'lost' off the West African coast.[4]

Georgoulis and his crew vehemently denied that the ship had been scuttled, or even that it had called at Durban, but the first major mistake in the *Salem* plot had been made. The tanker was not sent to the bottom of the sea without incident as its death throes came to be witnessed by the crew of the *British Trident*. Suspicions were aroused, and investigators were soon on the trail of the perpetrators. In May, Captain Taylor of the *British Trident* complained that the *Salem*'s owner had never thanked him for rescuing his seamen.[5] It was surely not intended as such but it turned out to be a most bitter irony for Fred Soudan.

As the *Salem*'s crew came ashore in Dakar, Senegal, port police were given cartons of cigarettes and an alleged bribe of $26,500. The Tunisians were fearful of not receiving their money, but their silence was essential. Georgoulis therefore called Mitakis, and a representative from Greece named Christos Hatzichristos then arrived with funds. On January 21, each Tunisian was given $10,000 in Swiss bank wrappers and the entire contingent was flown to Paris.[6]

43

Doubledealing

Even before the oil had arrived in Durban, Reidel and Soudan had quarrelled about the role of Seaton, the ownership of the oil, and the channels of communicating with the SFF. Reidel's direct contacts with the South Africans confused SFF officials, but they greatly angered Soudan who felt that he was being shoved aside. Reidel had telexed Naude on November 13 about the details of delivery and payment, but it was his December 10 telex (Soudan evidently received a copy) claiming ownership of the oil, and demanding payment to Beets Trading, that completely enraged Soudan and led him to telex Reidel that same day: 'Apparently you are trying to side track us and move directly which is definitely unacceptable. As you know we could have gone ahead with the deal without you but we did respect our relationship with you. In view of the above we are compelled to review our situation which we will when we meet again hopefully on a better friendly and more gentlemanly manner.'[7] Soudan then told the SFF to ignore Reidel's telex. Later, the partners became embroiled in a more serious controversy over the ship itself and it was to sour relations for about a month and produce a staggering and rather opaque series of paper transactions aimed at resolving their differences.

Soudan's contract with Northern Ships stipulated that he would have to pay for Oxford Shipping 'on or about December 27' and that he would have to arrange for the cession of his hull insurance. He failed to carry out this latter obligation and was warned on December 21 that he was violating the terms of his contract; he was also given a December 28 payment deadline.[8] Soudan did not respond quickly. Triandafilou and Avgerinos then declared him in breach of contract and did not even wait for their own deadline. On December 24, the shareholders of Oxford Shipping removed Fred Soudan and his wife from their positions and selected Triandafilou as president and Avgerinos as secretary-treasurer.[9] This internal coup was at once joined by Reidel. Soudan's cousin and attorney, Wahib Attar, told Reidel that same day that Soudan had not yet paid Northern Ships and did not legally own Oxford. This meant that the bareboat charter between Oxford and Shipomex could be jeopardized so, according to Reidel, he moved to protect that deal. He therefore

44

offered to pay the $300,000 which Soudan owed Northern Ships. Attar called the New York shippers and asked that the stock in Oxford be sold to Reidel rather than Soudan, and he indicated that Reidel really owned the ship anyway. According to Reidel's agreement with Soudan, he was to take over the *Salem*, so perhaps he believed that he was entitled to control of Oxford as well. Two days later, Reidel telexed Northern Ships with a definite commitment to buy Oxford's shares the following day. Wahib Attar was authorized to sign a memorandum of agreement, but Reidel's money did not arrive on time.[10] It may be true that Reidel was trying to protect the Shipomex deal, and it is surely possible that he was unaware of Soudan's contractual lack of obligation to pay for Oxford until about December 27. However, Reidel was also undermining Soudan's role as a shipowner, as securing control of Oxford Shipping would have made him owner of the *Salem*. He would only have had to spend $300,000, rather than the more than $11 million mentioned in his earlier purchase agreement with Soudan. The activities of Attar were also rather curious as he was Soudan's relative and had worked on his behalf for several months. Now he seemed to have thrown in his lot with Reidel against Soudan's better interests. According to American Polamax partner John Haddad, Soudan was concerned in late December 1979 that Attar had become too close to Reidel.[11]

Soudan fought to hold on to Oxford Shipping and tried to meet the December 28 payment deadline even though he had been removed from the company. At 3 or 4 in the morning on December 28, he called Triandafilou and asked how he should pay the $300,000. Triandafilou was probably expecting to receive that sum from Reidel, so he stalled Soudan and asked him to call back on December 31. Soudan couldn't find him that day and consistently failed to locate him through January 3.[12] As of December 28, Soudan had plenty of money, but Oxford Shipping and the *Salem* were slipping out of his control.

Soudan had promised to sell the *Salem* to Reidel once the oil had arrived in South Africa, and he was prepared to abide by this commitment. However, he was not going to let Reidel run off with the ship for only $300,000. On this most busy December 28, Soudan worked out his accounts with Reidel and almost $7 million remained to be paid by the Dutchman for the purchase of the tanker and various expenses related to its voyage to Durban. The sum had dropped more than $4 million since the November 25 agreement, largely because the money sent to Mercabank off the top of SFF's payment was credited to Reidel's share of the entire *Salem* venture.[13] This agreement was not carried out, as the financial web became even more entangled.

Reidel was close to gaining control of Oxford Shipping: $300,000 was forwarded to the Israel Discount Bank in New York on January 3, and he planned to complete his takeover the following day. Meanwhile, Northern Ships' counsel Gregory Ligelis had told Soudan's New York lawyer Zuhayr Moghrabi that the stock certificates put into escrow awaiting Soudan's payment had been returned to the sellers, Triandafilou and Avgerinos. Soudan jumped into action. On January 4 1980, Moghrabi filed a writ in New York State's Supreme Court calling for an injunction to block the transfer of Oxford Shipping. Triandafilou, Avgerinos, Ligelis and others were cited as defendants, but not Anton Reidel. Moghrabi was seeking to prevent the transfer of stock, the turning over of stock certificates, or the release to Northern Ships of the $300,000 in the Israel Discount Bank. He argued that Reidel was attempting to acquire Oxford Shipping for only $300,000, thus defrauding Soudan, as the company was worth $12.3 million since it owned the *Salem*.[14] Moghrabi was successful in getting an injunction, representing an important victory for Soudan. On the other hand, the secret oil delivery to Durban could no longer be covered up completely. Soudan's contract with Northern Ships had to be filed in court, and it indicated the existence of a telltale voyage to South Africa.

Soudan then temporarily moved to the offensive. On January 9, he applied in New York to Liberia's Deputy Commissioner of Maritime Affairs to have the *Salem* registered under a different company, Mota Holdings Ltd. This would have put the ship out of reach of Reidel, and perhaps would have saved Soudan the $300,000 he was supposed to pay to acquire Oxford Shipping. The Liberians realized that a controversy existed over the ownership of Oxford, the company owning the *Salem*, as they had already received Triandafilou's December 24 letter removing Soudan. They therefore acted warily and tried to get the matter straightened out. In addition, Northern Ships had secured a temporary restraining order preventing Soudan from transferring or selling the *Salem*. It had been notified by the Liberians of Soudan's transfer attempt, so Avgerinos had filed an affidavit on that same January 9 to block Soudan. He claimed that Soudan had not fulfilled his contractual obligations as he had failed to establish a letter of credit to cover the $300,000 he originally owed, he had not listed Northern Ships on the hull policy as co-assured, and he had tried to make his payment too late. Avgerinos successfully argued that the *Salem* was Oxford's only asset so the tanker's ownership would have to be determined before there could be any meaningful settlement regarding the rightful ownership of Oxford's shares.[15]

A summit conference of the main participants was held in New York (requesting a hearing in a Liberian court would have consumed considerable time) on January 11 1980 to reconcile the contesting parties and resolve the issue of who owned Oxford Shipping and the *Salem*. Soudan and Reidel were there, as were Triandafilou and Avgerinos of Northern Ships, their lawyer Gregory Ligelis, and Soudan's attorney Zuhayr Moghrabi. It was agreed that all stock in Oxford Shipping would be placed in Soudan's name and his check for $300,000 (dated January 4) was accepted as payment. Reidel was to get back the $300,000 he had deposited in a New York bank, and he did recoup this sum five days later. In a move probably aimed at sweetening the pot for Northern Ships and preventing any claim by that company for control of Oxford, Reidel and Soudan promised to give Triandafilou and Avgerinos $300,000 per voyage for the next five trips made by the *Salem*.[16] Technically, Soudan did not really own the *Salem* when it visited Durban, but he surely had become its undisputed owner prior to the January 17 scuttling. On January 15, Soudan forwarded two notarized statements to the Liberians indicating that the *Salem* belonged to him and that only he and his wife could sign for Oxford Shipping. He also sent telexes to his shipbroker John Masters and the SFF firing Reidel and Attar from American Polamax. The apparent intent was to prevent them from ever claiming that they represented Soudan.[17]

The issue of who owned the *Salem* had been resolved, but Soudan and Reidel had to recompute their own internal finances as their December 28 agreement had been based on Reidel's receipt of the tanker. On January 12, another convoluted deal was struck according to which Soudan came to owe Reidel a little more than $5 million. He was to repay the $3 million he had received at the end of December, plus more than $2 million extra. In effect, it was almost the reverse of the earlier

47

agreement. Soudan would obviously own the ship, despite the fact that this point was not explicitly mentioned. Four days later, Reidel was already asking Soudan to forward over $2 million, but there is no evidence that Soudan ever sent it or repaid the other $3 million.[18]

Once the *Salem* sank, Soudan notified Reidel and rancor again came to the surface. Reidel telexed back the next day indicating that Mitakis was arranging for lawyers to represent both Oxford and Shipomex. Soudan was highly upset as Oxford belonged to him, and he did not want Mitakis or Reidel to interfere with his company. Soudan then telexed back, pointedly sending a copy to Mitakis as well. He maintained that only he could handle the affairs of Oxford, and he complained that Shipomex had contacted his London insurance broker Lowndes Lambert representing itself as owner of the *Salem*. Soudan described such a step as very serious, and stated that many people could end up being hurt. He then rather bitterly added: 'Agree that coordination is essential but only thru me and my lawyers as a first step. If any further individual moves are made whether with the insurance co or any other, you can forget the word coordination partner.'[19]

Reidel and Soudan met in Zürich January 27-29 (Mitakis was there also) and seem to have patched up their differences. Investigations into the sinking of the *Salem* were already underway and they were being bombarded with questions from lawmen and the media. They decided to stick together, and Reidel even provided Soudan with $1.25 million in February, which he had owed him from the original SFF payment to Beets Trading. Whatever financial arrangements were made remain secret, but it appears that Soudan did not have to abide by the January 12 agreement, as the *Salem* had been lost. Soudan did not expect to receive the insurance for the hull, and he preferred money to a continuing claim on the vessel.[20] Five years later, Reidel loyally served as a trial witness in defence of Fred Soudan.

One other aspect of the Reidel-Soudan relationship requires further consideration. 'Bert Stein' was the official director of Shipomex, which had bareboat chartered the *Salem*. He was seen by crewmen in Piraeus, identified by an eyewitness in Zürich, and his existence cannot be questioned. He was not Anton Reidel, but there is circumstantial evidence indicating that Reidel (perhaps in collaboration with Mitakis) actually operated Shipomex during the *Salem* affair. Logistically, it would not have been too difficult as Reidel's office for Beets Trading was in Zug, only eighteen miles from the Shipomex office in Zürich. Already we have seen that Soudan's protest about Shipomex contacting his insurance broker was sent to Reidel, not 'Bert Stein.' Reidel also had mentioned that Mitakis was seeking legal representation for Shipomex. Other clues are also available. On December 12 1979, Soudan sent a telex to Shipomex and addressed it to Anton Reidel. A telex from Reidel to Northern Ships indicated that the Rotterdam trader represented both Beets and Shipomex. Moghrabi is also said to have told a South African investigator that Reidel owned Shipomex.[21] Furthermore, the January 12 Soudan-Reidel agreement seems to imply that the bareboat charter fees were payable from Reidel's side of the ledger.

Fallout

When the *Salem* slid beneath the surface of the Atlantic, Shell assumed that its entire cargo was aboard. However, it quickly grew suspicious. Observations by the crew of the *British Trident*, the lack of a large oil slick, the unusual route taken by the tanker, and the reports of delays caused by boiler problems all raised many questions, but the key revelation (probably evident to Shell by January 23) was that the *Salem* had called at Durban.[27] Nevertheless, Shell abided by the terms of its contract with Pontoil and paid it over $56 million on that date.

The flow of documents in the spot oil market cannot keep pace with the plethora of transactions, and payment generally does not take place until all of the paperwork is completed. Pontoil didn't even send its money to Kuwait until January 8, and the documents required for the Pontoil-Shell deal (including the insurance certificate) were not assembled until January 16. Shell did not receive them until January 18, the day after the sinking, and it then had to decide its course of action. Had Shell known that Shipomex had chartered the *Salem* prior to Pontoil, it probably would not have paid Pontoil. However, this vital fact had not yet surfaced.[23] Perhaps Shell could have refused to pay and then sued Pontoil on the ground that the oil it received had already been stolen in Kuwait when pumped aboard the *Salem*? Perhaps it could have tried to wash its hands of the whole affair by claiming that it had agreed to purchase the cargo on a cif basis, and that the oil therefore was not Shell's property since payment had not been made? On the other hand, Pontoil had acted correctly and was not involved in the diversion to South Africa or the suspected scuttling. Shell had a reputation to uphold within the industry, and it felt obligated to make payment despite its serious reservations about the circumstances surrounding its cargo loss. Shell was a huge corporation engaged in thousands of transactions and it couldn't afford to let this one case lead to accusations of bad faith. Shell therefore paid Pontoil; it also moved rapidly to recover its loss.[24]

Shell filed an insurance claim for its cargo but was unsuccessful as the underwriters opted to fight it. As will be seen, drawn-out litigation then followed. Shell also took legal steps against the Strategic Fuel Fund, which had received most of its stolen oil, and it managed to have one of Soudan's bank accounts in Switzerland frozen. It was unable to locate 'Bert Stein,' but a writ was served on Hasso Osterkamp.[25] On January 30, Shell filed a writ of summons in London's Admiralty Court against Fred Soudan. It sought damages for the loss of its cargo and charged Soudan with breach of contract, and/or dereliction of duty, and/or negligence. The case was transferred to the Commercial Court in July, and a court order of October 21 permitted Shell to amend the original writ. This was accomplished on October 30 1980. Shell inserted the value of its lost cargo and specifically accused Soudan of fraud by inserting the passage: 'Alternatively damages for conversion of the Plaintiff's said cargo and/or damages for fraud and/or conspiracy to defraud the Plaintiffs of the said cargo and/or its value.'[26] Shell did not follow through with this legal action, possibly because Soudan did not have the financial ability to compensate it for the cargo, but also because Shell was managing to retrieve some of its money by other means.

Pontoil certainly profited from the sale of its cargo to Shell, but it then suffered once Kuwaiti officials found out that their country's oil had been delivered to South Africa. Kuwait had endorsed the oil embargo and was clearly embarrassed by the episode. At first, it suspended sales to Pontoil. Then it cancelled contracts with the Italian firm and banned all future provision of oil. Kuwait also instituted a new policy according to which tankers had to list their destination and all intended ports of call. It was hoped that these measures would prevent any repetition of the diversion of its oil to South Africa.[27]

Pontoil never paid its charter fee to Oxford Shipping, which was to be routed to Shipomex. This was its legal right as the fee was due only upon delivery of the oil to its destination. The sale of the cargo to Shell had no impact on Pontoil's obligation, so the perpetrators of the *Salem* plot lost an opportunity to collect $1.8 million when they diverted the tanker to Durban. They probably realized their miscalculation on this score and this may explain Reidel's efforts to secure payment from Pontoil prematurely (which implied that the cargo was not expected to reach its destination).

A Matter of Policy

Fred Soudan was the beneficiary of the *Salem*'s hull insurance policy through his role as president of Oxford Shipping. At first, he had tried to have the insurance assigned to him as an individual, which would have meant that ownership of Oxford would not have been required for him to collect on the policy. This procedure was unacceptable in the insurance trade.[28] Soudan then arranged for a policy via Oxford and he clearly controlled that shipping company at the time of the *Salem*'s loss.

The *Salem* was insured under a one-year time policy and Soudan was required to pay quarterly premiums. Three-quarters of his coverage was through Lloyd's underwriters, but one quarter was placed in Norway where a slightly lower rate was obtained. The *Salem* had cost less than $12 million, but it was insured for $24 million. Was it overinsured as part of an insurance fraud scheme? Apparently not, as other vessels in its class were insured similarly. The *Salem* was declining in value due to ageing and the depressed shipping market of the late 1970s. It was worth no more than $12 million as a total loss, but the repair of serious damage could have cost considerably more as a result of extensive outlays for labor and parts. Underwriters wanted to make sure that the amount of coverage sufficiently covered such major repairs, and they also benefited from the higher premiums.[29]

How did Soudan manage to get insurance so easily, considering his complete lack of experience as a shipowner? From the perspective of the insurance broker, the ship was the main concern, not its owner. The *Salem* had an unblemished record as the *Sea Sovereign* and *South Sun* so there was no reason why it should not be insured. In regard to Soudan, it must be reiterated that he was introduced at Lowndes Lambert by John Masters, a respected shipbroker. In any case, insurance brokers were not too selective in 1979. The shipping boom of the early 1970s had generated increased insurance competition as new underwriters entered the field. They hoped to take advantage of the rising interest rates by investing their premiums, but they were soon faced with a depressed shipping market and low premium rates. Rate-cutting therefore increased, and greater risks were assumed, as a surplus of underwriters fought for a piece of the insurance pie at a time of declining profits. In fact, the potential for profit on policies was often of little concern as greater income could be secured by chanelling the premium cash flow into investment. Brokers were party to the same process as they lived off fees received from the underwriters, which were deducted from premium payments.[30]

Lloyd's of London is not a corporation, has no shareholders, and assumes no joint liability for policies. It is a society of underwriters organized into at least 370 syndicates, and it has about 46 member agents who don't belong to syndicates. Those seeking coverage approach a broker and never have direct contact with underwriters. The broker, through Lloyd's of London, finds underwriters willing to assume part of the risk at a given rate, and an insurance contract then becomes legally binding once an underwriter signs a broker's 'slip.' The policyholder then receives a 'cover note,' but generally is not given the actual policy until after the first premium is paid. In the *Salem* case, Soudan had a 'cover note' but was late in paying his first premium of almost $180,000. He waited until the South African payoff of December 28 and then forwarded his money on January 3. When the *Salem* sank, he did not yet have a policy, as it was issued three weeks later. However, his insurance coverage was nevertheless legally valid at the time of the loss.[31] Fred Soudan never paid his last three premiums as his ship was already beneath the Atlantic. Lowndes Lambert was therefore out a considerable sum (perhaps about $327,000) as a broker is obligated to pay all premiums to the underwriters even if it is unable to collect from the insured.

Evidence is rather sketchy on this point but it seems as if Soudan reacted to the news of the *Salem*'s demise by going to a Houston bank in an effort to secure a mortgage on the ship. According to the chief prosecuting attorney at his later trial, Soudan appeared at the bank on that fateful day but was unsuccessful in obtaining a mortgage as the ship had already sunk. Soudan's attempt to cash in immediately, rather than wait for possible insurance proceeds, was therefore made too late.[32] Soudan could surely have been at the bank that day, and it is clear that he knew of the *Salem*'s fate by 1 p.m. when he telexed Reidel. However, it was not positively established at his trial that Soudan had been at the bank that particular day, only some day about that time. In any case, Soudan certainly tried to mortgage his tanker, using the insurance 'cover note' as presumable proof of ownership. He may have feared that he would never be able to collect on his insurance, but he also may have been executing a slick move in which money could be acquired for a lost tanker and then used to cover his debt to Reidel.[33] Remember that Soudan's January 12 agreement called for the payment of several million dollars, and that Reidel had contacted him on January 16 to ask for his funds. This was the day before Soudan allegedly showed up at the bank.

Fred Soudan never filed a claim, even though his tanker had suffered a complete or 'actual total loss' (as compared to a 'constructive total loss' in which a ship is salvageable but no attempt is made as the cost of such an operation plus repairs exceeds the value of the vessel). Soudan realized that any claim would be challenged, as the circumstances were surely suspicious, and he also wanted to avoid prosecution for insurance fraud. He could only be charged with this offence if a claim was filed; otherwise, he could only be cited on the lesser charge of conspiracy to commit insurance fraud.[34] Conversely, not trying to collect the $24 million would make Soudan appear guilty as there was no precedent for the absence of a claim when coverage was so high.[35]

Faced with a no-win situation, Soudan tried to get rid of his policy. A lawyer was dispatched to London, where he spoke with representatives of Shell. He suggested that the hull policy could be assigned to Shell and that any insurance money received would be split. Shell therefore would have had an opportunity to recoup some of its loss on the stolen cargo, but it rejected this overture as unethical.[36] Soudan's lawyer also approached the

53

insurance broker Lowndes Lambert, attempting to cancel the policy and obtain a refund of the premium. Lowndes Lambert had actually thought of the same thing earlier, once it appeared that fraud had taken place, but the underwriters refused to cancel. The latter probably believed that they had a strong case in contesting any claim by Soudan, and they obviously did not want to part with their premiums. It was clearly their right as a broker may not cancel any policy without the consent of the underwriters. For its part, Lowndes Lambert was anxious to get off the hook as it owed premiums to the underwriters and expected that Soudan would no longer be making payments. Once Soudan's lawyer proposed a policy cancellation, Lowndes Lambert was obliged to say 'no.' Precedent was important, but it was also realized that Soudan was trying to avoid prosecution for insurance fraud. If the policy had been cancelled, then it would have been extremely difficult to maintain that a fraud had been perpetrated. Furthermore, Soudan had incurred a total loss and insurance guidelines would have rendered the return of premiums most unlikely under such circumstances.[37]

Soudan would have encountered several problems had he tried to collect on his insurance policy, even if no scuttling of the vessel had been proven. As the assured, it was his responsibility to inform the underwriters of all material facts prior to the issuance of a 'slip.' In at least two areas, Soudan seems to have been negligent and the underwriters could therefore have challenged any claim on the basis of concealed information. Soudan arranged a bareboat charter with Shipomex on November 25, prior to insuring the ship. This meant that Shipomex would be in control of the vessel but Soudan failed to report this vital detail to the insurers. In addition, insurance was contingent on the *Salem* being 'seaworthy,' a term incorporating the proper licensing of master, officers and crew. In fact, Georgoulis was unqualified to serve as master. Two other factors were really red herrings as far as hull insurance was concerned: the cargo fraud involving the delivery and sale of Shell's oil and the change in the *Salem*'s destination. The cargo had no legal connection to the hull and was insured separately. Destinations did not have to be reported as Soudan's policy was on a one-year time basis, rather than geared toward a specific voyage. It should be added that had Soudan's policy been deemed invalid due to concealment of information, he would not have been entitled to a refund of his premium.[38]

Fred Soudan worked hard to acquire the *Salem*, an asset worth more than $11 million. As a total loss, it was valued at $24 million, but it had become a soggy white elephant submerged beneath the sea. No claim was ever filed, and none is likely to succeed as the usual six-year statute of limitations has already expired.

The Unpointed Finger

The *Salem* was scuttled to cover up a cargo fraud, as Shell was soon going to realize that most of its oil had disappeared from the tanks. Once the *Salem* arrived at any port, Shell would surely have ascertained that the vessel was loaded with seawater. By sinking the ship, it may have been possible to fool Shell into believing that its entire cargo had been aboard. More problematic is the issue of when the decision to scuttle was made. Conclusive evidence is not available but it is conceivable that scuttling was not part of the original plan. Georgoulis made an interesting point at his appeals trial when he stated that it made no sense to hire him as master if scuttling had been on the agenda. Due to his lack of a master's certificate, a thorough investigation would surely have been initiated.[30] Georgoulis claimed that he was unaware of any scuttling plan until the *Salem* had offloaded its cargo in Durban, and that the crew was informed at the same time and given extra pay.[40] A plot could certainly have been hatched earlier without his knowledge but Georgoulis's account appears reasonable as far as his own role was concerned. It has been reported that he bought television sets for the tanker in the Gulf, an expense he may have forgone had he planned to sink the ship. He also telephoned a wine merchant in Genoa. What he said remains a mystery but perhaps he really was expecting to journey to Italy as Pontoil had intended?

Did Soudan and Reidel know about plans to scuttle the *Salem*? They have consistently denied any knowledge and an examination of their telexes just prior to and after the sinking reveals no intimations about the scuttling. The huge mass of materials gathered for Soudan's trial also failed to include any evidence that he or Reidel was involved. Soudan always brought up his

Corpus Christi scheme, even to his confidant John Haddad. Also revealing is the fact that spare parts purchased with the *Salem* (but available in Sweden as the vessel had been built there) were forwarded by air freight to Houston in anticipation of the tanker's arrival in Corpus Christi in late January. The telex to Sweden ordering this delivery was sent only thirteen days before the Salem sank.[41] One must additionally consider two other factors. Had Soudan planned a scuttling, he may have attempted to acquire a less costly voyage insurance policy for his ship rather than a time policy, and he probably would have made it to the bank to secure a mortgage before the *Salem* was already lost. In June 1980. Soudan offered to come to England with documents supposedly proving his innocence of the scuttling, demanding in return that he would not be arrested during his visit. Scotland Yard turned him down.[42]

Soudan and Reidel were working on new deals which all fell through as a result of the scuttling scandal. Reidel's telex the day before the sinking discussed financial arrangements for them, mentioning cement negotiations with Nigeria and an oil contract which had been settled upon with a 'government of our choice'. They were also planning to deliver more oil to South Africa, making Soudan particularly apprehensive that Shell's lawsuit against the SFF would reveal the cargo fraud that had been perpetrated.[43] The South Africans badly needed additional cargoes and had been cooperating with Soudan toward that end. He had indeed provided his first shipload of crude on schedule and SFF officials were unaware that the oil had actually belonged to Shell. Soudan had been searching for another tanker and he had decided to purchase the 228,000 deadweight ton *Norse King*. On January 23, the SFF's bank, Volkskas, telexed Mercabank to confirm that it had a deal with Soudan for a cargo to be delivered February 1-15. Mercabank then issued a letter of credit for $14 million, although it had already agreed to provide the funding before the *Salem* sank.[44] According to shipbroker John Masters, Soudan behaved very differently from the way he had when buying the *Salem*. In the previous situation, he seemed unconcerned about who would operate his ship and appeared to be acting on behalf of Reidel. In the *Norse King* negotiations, Soudan insisted that his ship be operated by a good company and acted as if he was really going to be the owner of the vessel.[45] After the *Salem* sank, SFF director Dirk Mostert investigated Soudan and gave him the go-ahead to provide more oil for South Africa.[46] However, the *Salem* affair had cast a pall over the negotiations and the letter of credit for the *Norse King* had already expired on February 12. Soudan did not follow through and his days as an oil broker were over. Ironically, the *Norse King* soon became active in breaking the oil embargo against South Africa. Owned by a Scandinavian firm, it reportedly delivered at least six cargoes between May 1980 and September 1981.[47]

Soudan could have been feigning, but it seems as if he was highly distressed by the sinking of his tanker. His motivation for seeking a mortgage is difficult to determine. However, his comments revealed great anxiety and he even appeared astonished that the *Salem* had been near the Senegalese coast. He thought it was heading for Corpus Christi.[48] Soudan publicly maintained that he had not been in control of the vessel when it was lost as he had bareboat chartered it to Shipomex. When John Masters called upon hearing of the sinking, Soudan said the same thing and acted surprised that the *Salem* had gone down.[49] Blaming the rather untraceable Shipomex company, headed by the pseudonymous 'Bert Stein,' may have been part of the original plan, but it was also possible that Soudan felt he was being left out to hang and dry. He was the registered owner of the *Salem* and would have to take all of the public and legal flak, while those Greeks actually responsible for the scuttling remained hidden in the wings. Soudan portrayed himself as a victim or patsy, and the memories of Reidel's effort to take over Oxford Shipping were fresh in his mind. He fumed: 'I am the one who has had injustice done. I intend to seek justice through all legal means.'[50]

Peter Griggs, Deputy Chief Superintendent of Scotland Yard's Fraud Squad, investigated the *Salem* case in great detail and arrived at the professional judgement that Soudan knew of an intended scuttling from the beginning.[51] Evidence can surely be gathered on this side of the ledger. For example, the Greek crewmen had so little luggage that the Tunisians had to loan them swimming trunks in both Dar es Salaam and Dubai.[52] This does not necessarily implicate Soudan but one must also consider that his Corpus Christi plan was completely unworkable as the *Salem* was too large to use that port. Perhaps this oversight may be attributed to Soudan's lack of knowledge about shipping, but why did Soudan fail to make any advance arrangements to receive the ship there if he really expected it to arrive in late January? Furthermore, the Corpus Christi paper-chase could conceivably have worked only if the perpetrators had possessed legal title to the oil offloaded in Durban. Since the oil had been owned by Shell, and was due to be delivered to France, the oil giant would certainly have blown the whistle once it found out (most likely from *Lloyd's Shipping Index*) that the *Salem* was heading westward across the Atlantic. Also consider that Reidel and Mitakis had claimed that the *Salem* was going to discharge its seawater in Milazzo, Sicily, not Corpus Christi. Early in December, Mitakis had even inquired about freight rates from Mina al-Ahmadi to Milazzo.[53] Another problem regards the *Norse King*. Soudan already owned the *Salem* so he would not have needed another tanker unless he had planned a large number of deliveries. No such contracts have been produced so it is possible that the *Norse King* was to be used once the *Salem* had been sunk. Another ingredient is the timing of negotiations in New York regarding who should own the *Salem* and Oxford Shipping. Was it a coincidence that an agreement was reached, and legal title assigned, less than two days before the scuttling? Lastly, one has to ponder the intricacies of the three Soudan-Reidel deals of November, December and January. Unfortunately, they do not shine any definitive light on this issue, but the last arrangement called for Soudan to pay Reidel over $5 million. Soudan didn't have that much money so he may have been expected to secure the remainder out of the proceeds from the hull insurance once the ship was scuttled. An alternative hypothesis would be that Soudan planned to repay Reidel in the course of transacting future commodity deals.

The *Salem* was surely scuttled, but the involvement of Soudan and Reidel remains questionable. Hull insurance fraud was not their major concern (cargoes had by then become more valuable than hulls) as they were just part of a larger conspiracy which was often beyond their comprehension and control. The order to scuttle probably came from Greece, as the payoff money for officers and crew definitely originated there. A pattern was evolving among Greek shippers in which cargo fraud and scuttling were often parts of the same operation. Gregorios Makrygiorgios was allegedly behind the strange demises of the *Brilliant* and *Alexandros K.* and it was not too surprising that he was named as a defendant in the *Salem* case. Maritime fraud was on the upsurge, and Greece was emerging as its command centre.

The twilight world

■ The *Salem* fraud was both intricate and audacious, but what conditions helped make it possible? Foremost among them was the depressed shipping market of the late 1970s, which led many desperate and previously legitimate entrepreneurs into the more lucrative sideline of maritime fraud. Antony Trew's *Death of a Supertanker*, a novel published in 1978, describes the rather harsh economic realities of the period and presents a fictionalized account of conspiracy and sabotage off the South African coast. Coinciding with the rising incidence of fraud was the Iranian revolution, which seriously disrupted the flow of oil to South Africa. A critical energy crisis resulted in 1979, which was compounded by Pretoria's continuing supply of oil products to the internationally embargoed regime in Rhodesia. South Africa's oil secrecy laws were tightened as part of an effort to cope with the emergency, and this blackout on information then created an atmosphere which served to attract those bent on subverting legal norms.

Times were turbulent as order was breaking down on many fronts. Terrorism was rampant, Lebanon had descended into the cauldron of internecine war, American hostages were being held in Iran, and Soviet troops were intervening in Afghanistan. On the economic front, the spiralling price of oil fuelled rampant inflation and interest rates soared. The best barometer of international apprehension and disquietude was the price of gold. It reached its historic peak of $875 per ounce in January 1980, the same month that the *Salem* disappeared beneath the waves.

The *Salem* case was typical neither of maritime fraud practices, nor of the means of securing oil for South Africa. Rather it was the boldest and most outrageous example, a graphic illustration of what the tumultuous times had spawned. It represented the culmination of a process, a last hurrah, for the situation was just beginning to return to greater tranquility. Trends had just started to reverse as the shipping industry rebounded, maritime fraud decreased, and South Africa's oil position became less precarious.

Ebb Tide

As the world economy was battered by stagflation, international commerce was forced to retrench. High prices drove down the demand for many commodities as people had to lower their economic expectations. Oil prices jumped to over $40 per barrel, sending thermostats downward and customers to dealers specializing in small cars. Alternative fuel sources were more extensively tapped, and oil conservation measures were introduced by government fiat. It had earlier been anticipated that world demand for oil would rise throughout the 1970s but, in fact, it began to fall.[1] Shippers were therefore confronted with decreasing demand for tankers, and higher fuel costs. The shipping industry's level of transactions is one of the best indicators of international economic trends as 'maritime transport and its associated activities form the world's biggest single business activity.'[2] In the late 1970s, the decline of shipping surely mirrored the broader distress of international markets at large.

Shipping had been doing very well indeed up to the end of 1974 as the demand for vessels was high. This led to the expansion of fleets, new construction orders, and the assumption of additional mortgage obligations. Governments also stepped in to provide subsidies for shipbuilders and shipowners. Then the axe fell as the dozen years of bounty were over: 'Marine historians may look back at 1975 as the year during which retribution – in the form of severe economic recession – inevitably followed the biggest shipbuilding boom ever known. Overtonnaging, particularly in the tanker trades, led to a serious falling-off in the demand for new ships.'[3] The surplus in shipping tonnage may be measured by a combination of several factors such as the number of vessels laid up, carrying less than a full load, spending excess time in port, cruising at slower than usual speeds, and experiencing other types of inefficient operation. By mid-1977, there was an overall surplus of 137.5 million deadweight tonnes, and the figure rose to 142 million a year later. The *Lloyd's Register of Shipping* annual report for 1978 bluntly declared: 'The situation for shipping is probably the grimmest in post-war history.'[4]

Tankers were particularly vulnerable. Demand for oil was down, and new production in the North Sea eliminated the need for many vessels that had previously supplied Britain and other states. In addition, the United States was increasingly turning toward a nearby supplier, Mexico, and exploiting its own reserves in Alaska. Consequently, tankers and combined carriers capable of transporting oil were frequently laid up. At the end of 1976, 32.1 million deadweight tonnes were suffering this fate. The figure then rose to 35.7 million in June 1977, 35.8 million in December 1977 and 48.5 million at midpoint 1978.[5] Tanker owners were confronted with low charter rates, the repayment of mortgages taken out in the happier days of the early 1970s, and increasing service-costs for maintenance and port charges. New orders were at their lowest level since 1967, and scrapping became a popular option among the desperate. In the first half of 1977, over 3.7 million deadweight tonnes were scrapped; in the corresponding period of 1978, the statistic jumped to almost 7.1 million.[6]

In 1979, presaging a general economic recovery throughout the Western world, the shipping industry came back from the doldrums. Orders for new vessels began to increase, with the level attained in 1980 being the highest since 1974. The tanker trade bounced back, with surplus tonnage dropping from 142 million deadweight tonnes in mid-1978 to 108.9 million by mid-1979. As of June 1979, only 17.9 million tonnes were laid up, a sharp decline from the 48.5 million evident two years earlier. Scrapping for the last half of 1978 exceeded 6.5 million tonnes, but was down to less than 4.2 million during the first six months of 1979.[7] The Iranian revolution, culminating in the Shah's departure for exile in January 1979 and the rise of Ayatollah Khomeini, contributed to the tanker resurgence. Although the supply of oil worldwide did not increase in 1979, and the price per barrel rose, more tankers were still needed and the spot charter rate almost tripled. Iran had a significant impact as its reduction in production buttressed the firmer crude oil price, and these factors encouraged countries outside the Middle East to increase their production. Inefficiency in these new oil operations, compounded by the decline of control by the major oil companies (especially in Iran itself), lead to loading difficulties and delays. Contributing to these latter problems was the huge increase in imports by Third World oil-exporting states, which produced long queues of vessels waiting to discharge their cargoes. Tankers were therefore wasting more time in port, and greater tonnage had to be available to transport the same quantity of oil. A tanker resurgence resulted, despite higher bunker prices and war-risk insurance premiums imposed after the outbreak of the Iran-Iraq conflict in September 1980.[8]

Troubled Waters

The shipping slump was accompanied by a rising incidence of casualties. The percentage of tonnage totally lost constantly increased during the period 1977-79, with 1979 setting a record of more than one-half per cent. Shipwrecks, sinkings and fires were plaguing the industry, especially in regard to vessels more than ten years old. As for tankers, 1979 marked the high point for casualty rates, as well as for major oil spillages.[9]

What produced this rash of casualties? In part, the trend toward larger vessels contributed to the problem as navigation charts for ships with such a deep draught were inadequate. Also, these behemoths were more difficult to handle and harder to salvage when in distress.[10] Another factor was that many shipowners tried to make it through the hard times by skimping on repairs and maintenance. Flags of convenience vessels were not as problematic as one may have assumed, despite their poor safety standards and the dubious qualifications of their officers. Such open registry was increasing as shipowners sought weaker regulations and lower fees. Liberia, with the world's largest merchant fleet in terms of tonnage, had only the third highest number of casualties. It had by far the most extensive flag of convenience fleet, but much of its tonnage was in the form of newer and relatively safer vessels. Liberia also controlled almost two-thirds of the flag of convenience tanker tonnage. It should be realized, however, that Liberia was only fifth in the number of registered ships so its incidence of casualties was still fairly high.[11]

A dramatic increase in fraud was partly responsible for escalating casualty rates. Normal rules of conduct were thrown to the wayside as shippers, economically battered, fought to keep their heads above water. Many resorted to cargo fraud, and then tried to cover up their transgressions by scuttling their ships as insurance payments were more lucrative than scrapping. Others turned to insurance fraud, intentionally damaging or sinking their vessels. Occasionally, both types of fraud were attempted on the same voyage. There was even an upsurge of piracy, particularly in Southeast Asia, off the West African coast, in the Eastern Mediterranean, and in the Arabian Sea.[12] These were surely dangerous times on the high seas, and within Lloyd's of London as well. As Godfrey Hodgson explained: 'What worried underwriters was not so much that the highest peacetime casualty rate in history coincided with an unprecedented wave of marine fraud; it was the fact that all of this happened at a time when, because of competition and undercutting, rates were disastrously low.'[13]

Accurate statistics on maritime fraud are not available for the late 1970s as there was no central monitoring agency, and suspected fraud is difficult to prove under any circumstances. Nevertheless, it was clearly rampant. In November 1979, the Eleventh Assembly of the Inter-Governmental Maritime Consultative Organization (IMCO) met in London and, for the first time, fraud was discussed. IMCO was a specialized agency of the United Nations, founded in 1958 to coordinate the exchange of information on maritime safety standards and shipping technology. States comprised its membership, and IMCO was later converted into the International Maritime Organization (IMO) in May 1982. Lebanon raised the fraud issue, and a resolution calling for cooperation to prevent the physical seizure of ships and cargoes was passed. Paper frauds were not included, but the organization then timidly called upon commercial interests to practice self-regulation whenever possible. There was clearly a fear of offending some member states, but at least the problem was recognized.[14]

Meanwhile, shipping and insurance interests were becoming alarmed and the Chief Constable of the Port of London Authority Police, Eric Ellen, was asked to investigate the increase in maritime fraud. The Institute of Chartered Shipbrokers, a British-based organization, was also concerned and it conducted a London seminar on the topic in May 1979. It was so oversubscribed that a larger facility was found, and still all those who wanted to attend could not be accommodated. A Fraud Prevention Committee was set up that year, and then another seminar was conducted in New York in June 1980. Pressure was building up to do something to combat fraud, with the major impetus being provided by Ellen's January 1980 report on his eighteen-month investigation. Ironically, Ellen's call for an international task force was made the day before the *Salem* sank.[15] He received strong backing from the International Chamber of Commerce, headquartered in Paris, and a decision was made in November of that year to found the International Maritime Bureau. In May 1981, it commenced operations in London. Eric Ellen was appointed its director. The IMB serves as a clearing-house for reports about fraudulent practices, investigates allegations, educates the public about maritime fraud, and develops new procedures to foil the fraudsters.

The fraud trail clearly led to Greece. Greek shippers had been hit particularly hard by the economic slump. They had invested heavily during the early 1970s and were experiencing difficulty in repaying their debts. Greek crews were also demanding higher wages, and the rising value of the yen was adding to shipbuilding costs as so many of Greece's ships were built in Japan. Furthermore, the Greek fleet received no government subsidies and could not easily compete with those of other states where such subsidies were prevalent, and even increasing. This assistance to many international shippers kept freight rates low as national prestige superseded profitability. The free-market Greeks therefore fell upon especially rough times, and many turned to fraud.[16]

Greece's merchant fleet was substantial, ranking fourth in the world in tonnage in 1977 behind Liberia, Japan and Britain, and passing the union jack the following year to move into third place. In addition, Greek shippers placed 30 per cent of their tonnage under flags of convenience, usually those of Liberia or Cyprus. Ships operating under the Greek flag had a dismal safety record during the late 1970s as they suffered the highest casualty rate of any fleet. In terms of total losses, the figures were truly abysmal. Measured by tonnage from July 1978 through June 1979, Greek tanker losses were 4.72 times the world average, dry bulk carriers 5.36 times, and general cargo carriers 3.20 times![17] Greek vessels were often old, but fraud surely accounted for much of the problem. An analysis of 93 fraud cases (involving one million dollars or more) up to November 1979 revealed that an amazing 46 of the ships flew the Greek flag! Sixteen sported the Cypriot flag, which was often used by Greek shippers. Only one was registered in Liberia. Most frauds were committed on smaller vessels, while ships in Liberia's fleet tended to be rather large.[18]

Greek shippers were running haywire, and their government did little to control the situation. Investigations into 24 cases of possible maritime fraud were conducted during the years 1977-79, but few prosecutions resulted. Greek authorities claimed that shippers, underwriters and receivers were reluctant to press charges.[19] In addition, cargoes diverted to Greece were frequently sold there legally as compliant judges issued title to dubiously obtained commodities. Piraeus became the hub of cargo fraud in the Mediterranean, and Greek shippers expanded their activities to Lebanon where militias controlled ports and great profits could be made by providing goods to embattled factions. This is what happened in the case of the *Alexandros K.*

Shipping casualties began to decrease by 1980 and, not surprisingly, so did maritime fraud. Lost tonnage set a percentage record of 0.54 in 1979, but dropped to 0.43 in 1980. In this latter year, the serious casualty rate for tankers was the lowest since 1974, and major oil spills fell to just over a third of the 1979 level. The crucial figures for Greek shipping also indicated a sharp decline in tonnage losses in all categories of vessels.[20] The prime reason for this reversal was that the shipping industry had emerged from its depression, enabling vessel owners again to seek their fortunes legitimately. International clamour about maritime fraud also had an effect as enforcement of the rules of the sea became more stringent and prosecutions became more common, even in Greece.

The *Salem* scuttling was rather typical as the ship was old, owned by a company not operating any other vessels, chartered by a name-plate firm with a mysterious director, and navigated by Greek officers.[21] It also sank as the first in a series of disastrous tanker accidents. Three of them involved ships which went down unloaded off Africa. On March 11 1980, the Spanish tanker *Maria Alejandra* sank off Mauritania, killing thirty-six crewmen. It was en route from Algeciras, Spain, to the Gulf.

April 3 turned out to be the most turbulent day of all as the *Mycene*, on its way from Genoa to Ras Tanura, sank near Senegal with one death. It flew a Liberian flag. Almost simultaneously, the *Albahaa B.* made its last gasps off the Tanzanian coast. The Liberian tanker had just delivered oil to Durban from Dubai. Six lives were lost. Coincidentally, the same firm that managed the *Albahaa B.* also operated the *Salem* when it was known as the *South Sun*.

It is unlikely that fraud was involved in any of these calamities, but suspicions still abound regarding the *Irenes Serenade*, which sank off the Greek coast on February 23. It was travelling from Turkey to Trieste, ostensibly with a full load of crude, and two seamen perished along with the vessel. Investigations are still taking place, but it seems as if this case bears many similarities to that of the *Salem*, especially regarding the unusually small oil slick created by the sinking. Rumours about the possibly missing cargo include many scenarios, including some claiming that the crude actually found its way to South Africa.[22]

The *Salem* affair was somewhat anomalous as it took place just when the prospects for shippers were brightening and frauds were decreasing. Its demise, and that of the *Irenes Serenade*, therefore represented the end of a calamitous maritime era. This is apparent in retrospect as one studies comparative statistics, but it was not readily evident at the time as the sinkings of the *Maria Alejandra, Mycene* and *Albahaa B.* seemed to form a pattern of continuing turbulence and skulduggery on the high seas.

Fuelling Apartheid

Mitakis intentionally targeted South Africa as the prospective purchaser of the *Salem*'s oil. He knew that few difficult questions would be asked, and that secrecy laws would help obscure the transaction, thereby protecting the perpetrators of cargo fraud. South Africa had been subjected to an embargo imposed by all OPEC states other than Iran since late 1973, but it had managed well nevertheless. Iran became its major supplier, and the increase in consumption was held down to perhaps only 4 per cent over a five-year period. Sufficient oil was available, but then the Iranian revolution led to a cutoff of deliveries. South Africa was in desperate straits, and 1979 proved to be its year of reckoning as it attempted to cope with a potentially catastrophic energy crisis.

South Africa was dependent on Iran for 90-96 per cent of its oil imports, and the Iranians also owned 17½ per cent of the shares in the Natref refinery. All of South Africa's refineries were geared toward handling Teheran's crude, so Iran's surging revolutionary situation in late 1978 had a disastrous impact on Pretoria's economy. By December 1, Iranian production had dropped from 6 million barrels per day to only 500,000 as labor unrest hit the oilfields. This created a shortage worldwide, making it extremely difficult for major oil companies to juggle their supplies in order to assist South Africa. In exile, Ayatollah Khomeini was calling for a ban on all oil exports, but the Shah persisted in delivering the limited quantities available. Then the weakening Shah tried to stem the tide by appointing Shapour Bakhtiar as prime minister, but the latter indicated (on January 11 1979) before the Shah even left for exile that no Iranian oil would be supplied to South Africa. The rising Islamic tide was surely making Iran more sympathetic to Arab concerns. As Khomeini gained control in February, this policy was reiterated and Pretoria was forced to bear the consequences.

At the time, South Africa was dependent on oil for only 20 per cent of its energy, but it had no domestic source of crude despite extensive exploration since the late 1960s. It had the most energy-intensive economy in the world based on energy consumed per unit of GNP, and its transport and military sectors were highly reliant on oil. Furthermore, its oil storage capacity outside the strategic reserves was limited, so imports had to be very closely coordinated with consumption.[23] South Africa was importing about 380,000 barrels per day of crude and 15,000 of oil products. It was also producing 20,000 barrels per day of products through its Sasol oil from coal process. Consumption may have been about 240,000; stockpiling in strategic reserves 70,000; exports to Rhodesia and other neighboring states 30,000; and bunkers provided to passing ships 50,000. The remainder was either lost during refining or used as a source of power for energy plants.[24]

In December 1978, South Africa reacted quickly to events in Iran by printing petrol rationing coupons. As expected, imports of oil early in 1979 were as low as 150,000 barrels per day, and the first quarter of the year showed a 40 per cent drop compared to the last quarter of 1978.[25] Although it is not clear if he was referring to this particular period, President Botha was later to say that 'there were times when it was reported to me that we had enough oil for only a week.'[26] South Africa responded to the emergency situation by not adding any of its imported crude to the strategic reserve. It also raised oil prices. On January 1 1980, a 10 per cent increase was put into effect, with the collected funds to be used for paying the bonuses needed to acquire imports. In February, petrol prices rose 18 per cent, with some of the revenue earmarked for the expansion of oil from coal operations. In June, the cost of petrol was raised 36 per cent, and that of kerosene 45 per cent. Speed limits were reduced and petrol stations closed on Saturdays.

These conservation measures were helpful, but much more was required. Spot market oil prices were moving upward, and suppliers were demanding huge premiums as they sought to take advantage of South Africa's weak position. Minister of Economic Affairs Chris Heunis revealed that some premiums paid were as high as 70 per cent over the normal world price of crude.[27] South African crude importers had been paying premiums for many years, but the demands were now becoming astronomical. The government therefore acted to encourage oil companies operating there to continue importing. An Equalization Fund, financed through oil purchase taxes, was set up to compensate companies by whatever amount their costs exceeded the official base price of crude. In addition, the companies were to receive an $8 per barrel subsidy.[28]

At first, South Africa had to scramble in the spot market to secure crude. This was purely a stop-gap measure as an effort was made to conclude long-term deals to replace those that had existed with Iran. As these contracts were worked out, John Deuss of the Netherlands (Transworld Oil) and Marc Rich of the United States (Minoil) became the leading suppliers, with Shell too playing a crucial role. For a while, an agreement with a Dane serving as Peru's honorary consul in Cape Town was also instrumental in acquiring oil from Oman.[29] In May 1979, the Conservatives swept to power in Britain and permitted North Sea oil to be sold to companies which were then able to free some of their own supply for delivery to South Africa. This swap arrangement was only temporary as there was much public clamour, leading Nigeria to nationalize the assets of British Petroleum in retaliation. Nigeria had already become disturbed by Pretoria's oil practices as, in March, it had prevented the *Jumbo Pioneer* from loading Nigerian crude for delivery to South Africa. The next month, it had seized the cargo of the South African tanker *Kulu* as it endeavoured to leave Nigeria with oil bound for Western Europe. Also interesting was South Africa's early 1979 agreement with the Caribbean island of Dominica. South Africa planned to construct a tanker terminal and refinery, and to run a free port area which could apparently be used for transshipping oil to Durban and Cape Town. The story was picked up by the media, riots ensued, and Prime Minister Patrick John was forced to resign in June.

It was impossible to shift to alternative fuels in the key areas of transport and the military, even though oil was in such short supply. Some thought was given to electric or hydrogen-powered vehicles, but they really did not offer a feasible solution. Oil remained essential so a decision was made in February 1979 to expand Sasol II, which was still under construction, and to build Sasol III. Coal, due to low labor costs, was cheap and plentiful, so converting it into oil seemed a sensible approach (In fact, oil companies were rewarded for acquiring crude for South Africa by being given contracts to export coal.) More research was encouraged into ethanol and methanol, which could be combined with petrol or diesel so as to reduce their usage. Ethanol could be derived from maize or sugar cane, while methanol was produced from coal, natural gas or wood. There was even a plea to farmers from the Minister of Agriculture to increase their acreage of sunflowers so that diesel fuel could be replaced with sunflower oil.[30] Another rather quixotic venture involved the so-called 'sniffer plane,' which presumably could fly over water and detect oil deposits. This project was being developed in France, but a South African oil exploration company was an investor. Not surprisingly, the 'sniffer plane' turned out to be a useless and fradulent hoax.[31]

A combination of conservation and aggressive purchasing of crude helped stabilize South Africa's oil situation by the middle of 1979. Rationing was never implemented, the sale of bunkers was not reduced, and oil was not taken out of the strategic reserves, which had been building up in disused Transvaal coalmines since 1966. Conditions remained serious, but not critical. In September, the order on reduced speed limits and no

Saturday petrol sales was rescinded. South Africa had bounced back, but at great expense. Sasol was not a cost-effective process, even at a time of soaring oil prices, as its rationale was strategic more than economic. The premiums paid for oil, and the subsidies furnished to importers, were also a financial drain. Nevertheless, South Africa could at least be consoled by the fact that gold prices were rising at a most convenient time.

Countering the oil embargo led to secrecy as security considerations required the protection of suppliers, shippers and importers who assisted the South African effort. Once the Arab states cut off deliveries in November 1973, Pretoria stopped publishing import statistics. The Petroleum Products Act of 1977 then introduced stringent controls over most information related to oil (the National Supplies Procurement Act of 1970 had already included some weaker clauses). Penalties of five years in gaol or a fine as high as 10,000 rands (a rand was worth slightly more than a dollar) were authorized. This act's provisions were then strengthened in June 1979, during the post-Iran crisis, and a penalty of seven years' imprisonment plus a 7,000 rand fine was specified. Enforcement even stretched to Jaap Marais, head of the Herstigte Nasionale Party, who in March 1981 publicly disclosed that petrol sales were being made to Zimbabwe. He was found guilty, but sentencing was waived.[3] In general, this oil secrecy legislation banned information about oil's production, transport, storage, quantity in stock, import or export. Oil companies operating in South Africa were forced to comply in order to maintain their right to conduct business there, although critics depicted this procedure as an excuse used by the companies to collaborate with the apartheid system. A black curtain descended over the subject of oil and, as will be discussed later, the media and some members of parliament began to question whether mismanagement was being concealed behind the professed concern for national security.

The *Salem* transaction thus was made under the protective cloak of secrecy. South Africa was bent on securing oil, and many unorthodox means had to be employed. Hiding them from any potentially prying eyes was deemed essential, so an environment of mystery and intrigue inevitably developed. Minister of Mineral and Energy Affairs Pietie du Plessis aptly remarked to South Africa's legislators: 'I want to challenge any honourable member in this House to try to purchase oil from an oil-producing country without entering the twilight world.'[33]

70

Circumvention

South Africa's secrecy laws went a long way in covering up oil import practices. Some information could be gleaned and extrapolated from Lloyd's publications, anti-apartheid organizations occasionally were able to gather some evidence, and seamen on tankers that discharged in South Africa were now and then known to reveal that hidden fact. Nevertheless, silence tended to prevail and the flow of oil was maintained. Monitoring of tanker movements was rudimentary at the time, and complicated by South Africa's refusal to list tankers that called at its ports. The Shipping Research Bureau in Amsterdam had not yet been established, and the countries under whose flags the tankers were operating had almost no interest in supervising the application of economic sanctions against Pretoria. Organizations that advocated sanctions, such as the United Nations General Assembly, the Organization of African Unity, and the Organization of Arab Petroleum Exporting Countries, lacked enforcement mechanisms. Those who assisted South Africa were therefore able to avoid most political embarrassment, or retaliation in the form of blacklisting.

The methods used to evade detection were often ingenious. The listing of false destinations was the norm, and certificates and documents were frequently altered or forged. Companies owning or operating the vessels were rendered difficult to trace as many were just post-box firms registered in places like Liberia or Panama. Masters of the tankers often kept two different sets of logbooks, and payment for delivery was typically through numbered accounts in Switzerland. Several means were used to obscure the origin of the oil. 'Multi-porting' involved picking up parts of the cargo at several terminals, thereby blending them. The same result was also achieved by having a vessel discharge oil into a partially loaded tanker while at sea. 'Topping' was a scam in which port personnel would falsify records to cover up the theft of oil. After oil was pumped aboard a ship, a greater quantity would be written into the books. Gradually, the paperwork would conceal the expropriation of enough oil to comprise an entire cargo, and it would be sent to South Africa with no record that it had ever been loaded. 'Topping' could also be accomplished by loading more

71

than the listed quantity. After several such loadings, the oil company receiving the crude would have enough partial loads stored up to deliver a full cargo to South Africa. Transshipment at sea also made it difficult to trace the cargo, as oil was transferred to a waiting empty tanker. Similarly, oil could be placed in storage tanks at Rotterdam, Singapore or the Netherlands Antilles and then discharged into different vessels for delivery to Durban or Cape Town. Another method was to have ships feign distress while off the South African coast. Their oil would then be pumped into other tankers and taken ashore.

On the way to South Africa, tankers had to be discreet in regard to radio contact. Some preferred no radio communication at all, while others used code letters and numbers in lieu of their appropriate names. Concealing the names painted on the vessels was also important. They could be painted out, covered with tarpaulins, or changed. After leaving South Africa, further attempts occasionally were made to hide the delivery. One means was to keep a small quantity of oil aboard, bring it to a refinery, and receive false certification that a greater amount of oil had been discharged. Another, known as 'double-loading,' was to continue toward Europe, pick up a cargo in Nigeria, and then proceed to the original destination as if no delivery had ever been made in South Africa. The most dramatic was scuttling.

Sanctions bred sophisticated subterfuges to circumvent them, and the potential for fraud was clearly evident.[34] In August 1979, representatives of international oil companies operating in South Africa sent a letter to a government official warning that fraud was probably due to 'an abnormal risk directly related to the current *modus operandi* of our crude importers.' They pointed out that protective insurance could be obtained, but this would require revelations about South African oil procedures. It was therefore advised that assuming the risk of fraud was preferable to undermining the national interest through contravention of the oil secrecy laws.[35]

South Africa's Strategic Fuel Fund was an attractive target for fraud because it failed to act defensively by establishing controls that would enhance its security. Quite to the contrary, it was less than scrupulous in its procedures and its choice of business partners, as turning a blind eye was deemed necessary to acquire oil under the embargo conditions. Proper documentation was not required and the background of suppliers was not investigated. Corruption internally was also possible as trans-actions were not carefully monitored by outside auditors and there was no separation of duties between those recording deals and those transferring assets.[36] Whether any SFF officials violated the law may never be known. In 1984, the Advocate-General reported: 'From the information at my disposal concerning the *Salem* case it does appear as if certain persons might well have been improperly enriched at the expense of the State, but I did not deem it advisable or necessary to investigate the matter further since it is already in the hands of the Attorney-General of the Cape with a view to possible criminal prosecutions.'[37] No charges have ever been filed, but there is some ground for suspicion as Anton Reidel has claimed that two Greeks took $1.6 million from the *Salem* payoff to South Africa.[38] Another clue may be found in the fact that the SFF was removed from the control of Sasol in March 1984 and placed under the administra-tion of the Industrial Development Corporation.

Eric Ellen and Donald Campbell have categorized four main types of maritime fraud: documentary, charter, scuttling and cargo.[39] All were integral components of the *Salem* case. In addition, at least six techniques used in undermining the oil embargo were evident (falsification of papers, coded radio contact, name change, post-box companies, Swiss bank accounts, and bribery of the crew). Two others are also pertinent. Soudan often discussed the phoney certification that could be obtained from a refinery in Corpus Christi, but this device was not actually used. Reidel claimed that the oil on board had been obtained through 'topping,' but it is highly unlikely that this could have taken place.[40] The plan had always been to load Saudi crude, indicating that any 'topping' would have had to take place at the Ras Tanura terminal. The switch to Kuwait came about suddenly and there was surely no time to perpetrate a 'topping' scheme there as well. Furthermore, the oil pumped into the *Salem* was carefully documented as belonging to Pontoil.

South Africa helped develop the means for its own sustenance, but they turned into instruments for its victimization. In a moral sense, some may attribute this to just retribution. In a criminal sense, it was maritime fraud.

Following the trail

■ Numerous investigations followed in the wake of the *Salem*'s demise. First to seize the initiative were those with a financial stake as they sought to protect their interests. The media, scenting a good story, quickly joined in and the more deliberate legal authorities also began their painstaking assessment. The centre of activity was London as the hull and cargo insurance had been placed there, and Shell International Petroleum was headquartered on the South Bank. From the perspective of law enforcement, it was therefore not surprising that Scotland Yard took the lead in pressing the *Salem* case even though none of the perpetrators were British. Greece, the Netherlands and the United States lagged far behind.

Sifting the Clues

The *Salem* was a total loss, so insurance investigators were immediately called upon to look into the sinking. The Salvage Association, which is closely associated with Lloyd's, arranged for Robert Bishop to handle the cargo insurance investigation and John Swan the hull insurance investigation. Fraud was deeply suspected as the explosions described by the *Salem*'s crew would not have been possible in a fully loaded tanker, and the oil slick was far too small. Bishop's search for information was more extensive than Swan's and it was ascertained within a week that most of the cargo had been discharged in Durban. On January 22 or 23, a source close to Bishop's investigation notified Shell of the fate of its oil. On February 2, South Africa's

Minister of Trade and Commerce, Schalk von der Merwe, publicly admitted that the *Salem*'s cargo had indeed been delivered there.

Bishop and four assistants carried out a seven-week investigation which included visits to Greece, the Netherlands, the United States, France, West Germany, South Africa, Senegal, Liberia, Kuwait and Dubai.[1] Extensive evidence was gathered and a three-hundred page report prepared. Fraud had clearly taken place and the cargo insurers got ready to challenge Shell's claim in court. Meanwhile, the hull insurance investigators had come up with a major break in the case. A Tunisian seaman who had sailed on the *Salem*'s final voyage decided to talk and verified that the cargo had been discharged in Durban. More importantly, he claimed that the tanker had been scuttled and hush money had been given to the crew. According to the seaman, the radio operator had not sent out a distress call before abandoning ship, nor had he sought to communicate with other vessels from the lifeboat until the *British Trident* had arrived. He also said that no explosions had taken place aboard the *Salem*, but his account of the amount of time spent in the lifeboats coincided with that of Georgoulis.[2]

At age 48, the seaman who refused to maintain his silence was by far the oldest Tunisian aboard the tanker. Upon arriving in Paris, he had attempted to find the insurers of the *Salem*, as he mistakenly believed that the hull insurance had been placed in France. Upon learning that most of the insurance had been underwritten in London, he went to the British embassy and began to tell his story. He had been angered by the treatment received on the voyage and had chosen to cooperate with the investigation. Among his complaints was that he had been given hardly any spending money in Malta and Tanzania, the crew had not been permitted to go ashore in Durban while the master had stayed at a hotel, and that the payoff money had not been sufficient. He had also been very upset by the scuttling arrangements. He was wary about setting off in a lifeboat and particularly concerned that a colleague with a heart problem was forced to undergo such an ordeal. He told about the intimidation of the Tunisians and his fears that they would be thrown out of the lifeboats if they didn't comply with instructions. The situation had been so tense that the Tunisians hid knives for possible use against the Greeks. After revealing many details about the *Salem* conspiracy, the Tunisian seaman received protection from the insurers as threats from Greece were made against his life.[3]

Most persistent of the journalists covering the *Salem* affair was Barbara Conway of the *Daily Telegraph*. She was a specialist in the area of fraud and was then at work on a book dealing with piracy. Sources in the Middle East had tipped her off that a major fraud was anticipated so she was already on high alert when the sinking of the *Salem* was reported in *Lloyd's List*. What struck her as curious about the initial reports was the absence of speculation regarding a conceivably devastating oil slick, even though 196,000 tonnes of oil were supposedly aboard the vessel. The Senegalese coast should have been threatened with a serious disaster, so Conway rightfully surmised that all of this oil could not have been in the tanks. Through a contact in the port of Dakar, she learned that helicopter surveillance of the slick had revealed it to be of little depth so she began to investigate the mystery of the *Salem* and provided British readers with most of their early knowledge about the case.[4] Also noteworthy was the research done by Nigel Ash, which culminated quite speedily in the publication of an excellent magazine article. Conway, and reportedly Ash as well, then contributed information to the BBC television documentary on the *Salem*, produced by David Darlow and broadcast on August 18 1980.[5] The common thread in all of these endeavours was that the key to the *Salem* conspiracy lay in Greece, and that Soudan, Reidel and Mitakis were only the front men for a very extensive plot. These representatives of the media had indeed headed along the correct trail.

Revelations by the Tunisian seaman pointed to criminal liability, so Scotland Yard sprang into action on the last day of January. Deputy Chief Superintendent Peter Griggs of the Fraud Squad took charge and investigators fanned out to Greece, the Netherlands, West Germany, Switzerland, Liberia and South Africa. There was harmonious collaboration with Liberia's investigators, but the South Africans were generally obstructive. Citing oil secrecy laws, they prevented Griggs's examination of most of the pertinent documents and often insisted that statements by its officials be made in Afrikaans rather than English. He did, however, get to see bank records and his sleuthing in South Africa in late February produced the evidence needed to undercut severely the claims of the perpetrators that the *Salem* had not been there.[6] For example, there was a receipt signed by Georgoulis indicating that he had stayed at Durban's Royal Hotel. There was also a record of Georgoulis's use of helicopters to travel from ship to shore, as well as the medical record of a Tunisian crewman who was treated for a suspected heart attack. In addition, there was proof that the electrician's wife, Maria Papaleon, had resided at the Parkview Hotel while the *Salem* was in port and had then flown to Greece. It was also ascertained that Georgoulis had telephoned Reidel in Switzerland (where Mitakis was also present) and had signed for the delivery of food and supplies for the ship. Griggs was not permitted to see the most pointed document of all, a January 29 statement by Freightmarine Shipping Ltd. This firm had handled the *Salem*'s port visit and it certified that the tanker had arrived on December 27, discharged oil, and departed on January 2.[7]

The Scotland Yard investigation was undertaken for the purpose of considering criminal prosecutions and was therefore quite distinct from the insurance investigations which were concerned with the validity of claims. Strangely, there was almost no contact between them and Griggs had to doubletrack over much of Bishop's investigative route. Griggs was given a copy of the Tunisian's statement but was not able to question him despite the seaman's visit to London. As legal evidence, this statement was highly questionable, as Scotland Yard could not verify that it was made by the man in question. In addition, the copy was in English but the seaman's account had probably been presented in either Arabic or French.[8]

Scotland Yard gathered sufficient evidence to seek prosecution, and its legal adviser indicated that charges of fraud could be substantiated. Then this recommendation was reversed and only charges of conspiracy to commit fraud were levied. This turnaround was most significant as fraud was an extraditable offense, whereas mere conspiracy was not. It was therefore most unlikely that those charged would ever be brought before a British court as all were foreign nationals. The issuance of arrest warrants could thus be viewed as an act of deterrence, a warning to fraudsters that Britain would not turn a blind eye to their machinations, rather than a serious effort at law enforcement.[9] To some, the warrants were even viewed as an attempt to gag the press as a chilling effect was cast upon the case in order to ensure fair trials for the accused. A technical shipping publication, upon advice of counsel, therefore decided not to publish an interview it had secured with Georgoulis.[10]

Britain was not very anxious to prosecute the *Salem* fraudsters as a great sum would be expended to seek conviction of non-citizens who carried out their plot within other jurisdictions. Nevertheless, there were also some important legal implications. Britain's standing in the case derived in the main from the placement of insurance coverage, and Fred Soudan had not filed any claim on the hull. Consequently, he and his cohorts could only be charged with conspiracy to commit fraud, not fraud itself. To sustain the latter charge, a fraud involving the cargo would have to be proven, but this necessitated a demonstration that part of the fraud was committed within Britain. The fact that Shell was a British company was not sufficient to determine jurisdiction. Following this approach, it could have been argued that the purchase of the ship and insurance took place in Britain and that these acts were integrally related to the ensuing cargo fraud. The prosecutors opted not to proceed in this direction, nor to consider pressing receipt of stolen property charges against the SFF.

Consequently, the arrest warrants issued on August 4 1980 (approved by Attorney-General Sir Michael Havers) charged two counts of conspiracy. One dealt with the diversion and sale of the cargo. Shell was not mentioned, but the warrant cited a plan 'to defraud such persons in UK.' The second charge was related to the scuttling of the vessel in an effort to secure insurance money. Mitakis was not named due to a lack of sufficient evidence, so the warrant cited Soudan, Reidel, Georgoulis and a gentleman named Locks.

There was some confusion about the exact identity of Locks as his forename was referred to variously as Johannes or Thomas Jurgen, but the main point was that he was deemed to be the elusive 'Bert Stein.' Locks, a thirty-three-year-old businessman in Frankfurt, strenuously denied that he was 'Stein' and there was no attempt by the West German authorities to investigate his role in the *Salem* affair. However, a photo of Locks said to have been supplied from West German police files appears to be the same man whose picture is affixed to 'Stein's' passport, and there are similarities in the handwriting of Locks and 'Stein.' 'Stein's' Zürich landlady recognized the face in Locks' alleged police file photo as that of her former tenant, but the person who probably could have cleared up much of the 'Stein' mystery was not willing to do so. Hasso Osterkamp claimed that he had known 'Stein' for four years; Locks said that he had been acquainted with Osterkamp for fifteen years and he admitted visiting him in Switzerland in December 1979, purportedly in regard to the purchase of an antique clock.[11]

Were Locks and 'Stein' indeed the same man? British and Greek prosecutors came to that conclusion and it seems to be valid. Nevertheless, numerous complications have clouded the issue. The names 'Thomas Locks,' 'Hans Locks' and 'Norbert Ginkel' all appear on a list dated February 2 1979. It was compiled by maritime fraud investigators and includes those suspected of involvement in illegal activities. 'Hans Locks' presumably refers to the father of 'Thomas.' Born in 1927, he is also known as 'Hannes' or 'Hermann Johann Locks.' 'Norbert Ginkel' was an associate of the junior Locks, and it is claimed that a shipping fraud investigation in August-September 1978 included an examination of their roles. The senior Locks was also implicated in this case where the cargo of a ship disappeared and the master blamed a supposed fire on board.[12] Some sleuths believed that the younger Locks and Ginkel were actually one person and, even after the sinking of the *Salem*, there was conjecture that Ginkel was 'Stein.'[13] Adding to the confusion was the allegation that several people had posed as 'Bert Stein' at various times, with the younger Locks being just one of them.[14] Anton Reidel had acted on behalf of Shipomex, 'Stein's' company, but it is highly unlikely that he had ever used the 'Stein' passport as he was too old to pass as having been born in May 1945, the date listed in the passport. On the other hand, that date suited Locks, who was born in 1947.

A Greek court convicted Thomas Jurgen Locks in absentia, adjudging him to be 'Stein'. There are also reports linking Locks to Greeks connected to the *Salem* affair, most probably Nick Makris, and seven phone calls to him were allegedly made on December 10 1979 from Afentakis's room at the Rotary Hotel in Geneva. Calls were also made that same day to Mitakis.[15] If he is not 'Stein,' Locks' reputation and business prospects have surely suffered unnecessarily, as he has cited the negative effects of the 'Stein' allegations on his deal with a commodities trading firm in Dubai.

As Locks junior continues his trading operations, part of the 'Stein' mystery remains. How much did 'Stein' get paid for his role in the *Salem* affair? Were these funds distributed out of the amount retained by Reidel from the original split?[16] Also curious is Fred Soudan's stay at Frankfurt's Holiday Inn on February 16 1980. Was he there to contact Locks?

The West African Connection

The *Salem* went down about ninety-four miles from the Senegalese coast, but the West African nation made no effort to claim jurisdiction. Its investigatory capacity was very limited and any attempt to delve into the case would have been costly. Senegalese nationals had no involvement in the *Salem* affair, so why should resources be wasted on an investigation? Of more direct concern was the possibility of pollution damage. A slick of twenty-four miles by five miles had developed and Senegal insisted on an indemnity to cover cleanup expenses. Simon Boissy, Director of the Merchant Marine, indicated that the passports of Georgoulis and Kalomiropoulos would be returned only if such a guarantee was received. It soon was, as Liberia assured Senegal that pollution cleanup costs would be covered by international conventions and Protection and Indemnity insurance.[17] Actually, the slick never seriously threatened the shore and there was no coastal damage at all. The quantity of oil which oozed out of the stricken tanker was obviously limited, as the bulk of the cargo had already been discharged in Durban.

The *Salem*'s crew had come ashore in Dakar and most members were quickly flown on to Greece or France. Six were detained temporarily, but four were then released on January 29 after a plea from Liberia's Deputy Commissioner of Maritime Affairs J.C. Montgomery. This left in custody the master, Georgoulis, and the chief engineer, Kalomiropoulos. They were being held until the pollution indemnity was provided, but it appeared that they would soon be dispatched to Greece to be questioned by Liberian maritime authorities. Their stay in Dakar then became longer than anticipated as Liberia began legal steps to seek their extradition. The *Salem* had flown the Liberian flag, so Monrovia's jurisdictional rights were clearly evident.

There was no extradition treaty between Liberia and Senegal but Liberian president William Tolbert was determined to seek prosecution of Georgoulis and Kalomiropoulos in order to improve his country's maritime image. He was Chairman of the Organization of African Unity and had been stung at the July 1979 OAU summit conference by criticism over the use of Liberian tankers in the South African oil trade. Tolbert moved decisively and, accompanied by Commissioner of Maritime Affairs Gerald Cooper, he travelled to Dakar to meet with Senegalese president Leopold Senghor. Extradition on the basis of an 1865 agreement between Liberia and Senegal's former French colonial administration was discussed as agreements made by France preceding Senegal's independence were deemed valid in the absence of subsequent replacements. In addition, the two countries gave strong consideration to proceeding on the basis of a direct request from one chief of state to another should any legal difficulties arise over implementation of the French-Liberian agreement. Such a request could have been made under the 'comity of nations' principle in an effort to further the application of international law, but this course of action was not needed, as the 1865 agreement proved sufficient.[18]

Joseph Chesson, Liberia's Minister of Justice, arrived in Dakar on February 9 and formal papers were served on February 19. By then, Senegal had concluded that the *Salem*'s listed cargo was not aboard, so ample grounds existed for honouring Liberia's request. On February 23 a court order in Dakar granted the extradition on the ground of falsification of documents; Georgoulis and Kalomiropoulos were then dispatched to Liberia on March 7. Senegal had completed its role in the *Salem* affair, but Liberia was still deeply involved. On March 8 the two Greeks appeared before Chesson and were informed of the criminal charges that could be levied against them: falsification of documents, theft of property, and criminal mischief in the form of scuttling. They faced possible ten-year terms, $10,000 fines, or both, but the Greeks steadfastly maintained their innocence. Criminal charges were never formally filed, and there was no indictment despite one court appearance made on May 2. A major stumbling block was that the two officers had been extradited from Senegal on the basis of only one charge, as sufficient evidence pertaining to theft of the oil and scuttling was not yet available at that time. Were they to be prosecuted on charges not listed in the extradition request, their defence attorneys would have had strong justification in challenging the procedure. On the other hand, non-criminal charges related to maritime code violations were officially registered. On March 14, Georgoulis was accused of acting as a ship's master without a valid license, operating a vessel without sufficient licensed officers, and operating it without sufficient licensed engineers. Kalomiropoulos, the chief engineer, faced only the latter charge.[19]

Liberia conducted an exhaustive investigation into the *Salem* affair. It administered the world's largest merchant fleet and had an extensive infrastructure prepared to deal with the loss of its vessels. Its operatives were unable to dive down to the *Salem*'s hull, as it was resting too far beneath the surface. Examining it with television scanners also proved impossible for the same reason. Nevertheless, the rather thin oil slick could be analyzed, and revelations that the tanker had called at Durban made investigators highly suspicious. Liberia's maritime offices in Greece, Britain and the United States went to work, and there was close collaboration with Scotland Yard. Anastasios Tzamtzis, the marine safety officer in Piraeus, interviewed eleven Greek crewmen and one Tunisian. David Bruce, his London counterpart, questioned four officers and two deck cadets from the *British Trident* and J.C. Montgomery quizzed Georgoulis in Dakar. Significant roles were also played by Solicitor-General E. Winfred Smallwood, Sr, who went to London, and by Alister Crombie, who was based in Reston, Virginia.[20] Montgomery predicted that the imprisoned Greeks would remain in gaol for at least twenty-five years, while Smallwood stressed Liberia's interest in strongly prosecuting the case: 'Every Liberian flag ship is by its very incorporation legal territory of the Republic of Liberia and as such subject to Liberian law. It is our absolute determination that all alleged criminal activities on board our ships will be thoroughly investigated and if as a result of that investigation criminal activity is established, the culprits will be brought to justice within a reasonable period of time. The matter of the *Salem* is of the highest priority to my Government.'[21]

The Liberian investigators completed their interim report in April 1980, concluding that foul play had indeed been committed. They recommended to the Minister of Justice that Georgoulis be prosecuted for his lack of a master's license, operating a vessel without properly qualified mates and engineers, and scuttling. Kalomiropoulos was to be cited for operating without licensed engineers and scuttling.[22] This report was never published, as internal Liberian politics came to have a dramatic impact on the case.

On April 12, a military uprising brought down the government of William Tolbert, and Master Sergeant Samuel Doe was installed as the new president. Joseph Chesson was among those executed by the new regime. The Commissioner of Maritime Affairs, Gerald Cooper, was retained, as Liberia sought to assure shippers that their interests would not be negatively affected by the new rulers. Cooper had served for five years, held ministerial rank, and was a respected figure in international shipping circles. Perry Zulu, the Minister of Finance, indicated that maritime policies would remain unchanged, but the commercial world had become jittery as there was fear that the system of open registry would be discontinued.[23]

Shipping was of great importance in Liberia as registration fees in 1979 had amounted to $13 million. These fees were the largest earner of foreign exchange for the economically hard-pressed nation, so flag of convenience registration was maintained by Doe. This step was not sufficient to quell the international sense of alarm and the number of ships registered dropped considerably. Political instability in Liberia had made it more difficult for shippers using its open registry to obtain shipbuilding loans from the international banking community, but the expected increase in Liberia's fees was also a relevant factor. Tolbert's government had already proposed such a raise, the first since the open registry system was inaugurated in 1949, and the Doe regime basically adhered to the Tolbert formula. The tonnage tax was tripled, with additional increases to be made through 1985. Some shippers preferred to go elsewhere, but the higher fees received by Liberia more than compensated for the smaller number of ships registered.[24]

Despite the demise of Chesson, Liberia continued to press the *Salem* case under Doe's military government. Newly appointed Minister of Justice Chea Cheapoo asked Shell to provide additional evidence, and a Commission of Inquiry was appointed which included Gerald Cooper. Extensive testimony was gathered at its May hearings, and among those presenting evidence were Georgoulis and Kalomiropoulos.

The defence of the master and chief engineer had gotten underway while they were still in Senegal, as a Greek lawyer named John Katsieris came to their assistance. He then went to Monrovia on March 8 and was soon joined by an associate,

Nikolaos Theodossiu. They made little progress on behalf of their clients, but a senior member of their firm, George Alfantakis, arrived on April 22 and considerable activity was generated. Alfantakis ostentatiously wandered around the Liberian capital in a white silk suit, and he was usually accompanied by bodyguards. At a time of extreme danger following the coup, he was quite conspicuous, while most Liberians were circumspect. Alfantakis referred to himself as 'Defender of Greek Military People' as he tried to curry favor with Doe's government. In a letter to the Liberian president, he appealed to him as 'one big and real soldier' and claimed that he had served as Vice-President and Minister of Defence in the Greek military government of 1974.[25] Actually, he had not been a member of the Greek cabinet, but he was the attorney for sixteen officers arrested in 1975 for conspiring against the new civilian administration. Alfantakis maintained that they were innocent and had been entrapped, and these comments led to a ten-month sentence for 'spreading rumours likely to cause anxiety' and 'insulting the leadership of the armed forces.'[26] Alfantakis also professed that Greek Minister of Justice George Stamatis had asked him to appeal to Liberia on behalf of Georgoulis and Kalomiropoulos. This claim was not corroborated by any documentation, but it is clear that the Piraeus public prosecutor brought theft and embezzlement charges against him in the spring of 1980 due to alleged links to a cargo fraud in September 1979. It involved the Cypriot freighter *Creon* and the cargo was sold in Lebanon.[27]

Alfantakis sent two letters to Minister of Justice Cheapoo and one to President Doe. He also secured a statement from Georgoulis's wife and Kalomiropoulos's brother and gathered letters to himself from the two accused *Salem* participants. In addition, he testified before the Commission of Inquiry. Alfantakis's defence of his fellow Greeks was based on three main arguments. First, he asserted that the extradition from Senegal had been illegal as there wasn't any valid extradition treaty. Furthermore, Alfantakis claimed that the Liberian registry of the *Salem* expired on March 3, four days before Georgoulis and Kalomiropoulos were flown to Liberia. Secondly, he charged that they were being illegally detained in an effort to extract payoff money. They could not legitimately be held so long without being indicted and they should have been released by President Doe's amnesty order affecting prisoners not being held for murder. Their names were on the amnesty list and their continued retention in gaol was a violation of President Doe's explicit orders. Thirdly, Alfantakis maintained that Georgoulis and Kalomiropoulos were being victimized for failure to pay sufficient bribe money. Singled out for particular criticism was J.C. Montgomery, Deputy Commissioner of Maritime Affairs. He was accused (although no corroborating evidence was provided) of taking $9700 from Georgoulis in Dakar, plus a plane ticket to visit Madrid. He also was alleged to have received an additional $4500 as a 'loan' to Minister of Justice Chesson. Montgomery was also said to have steered the defendants to a lawyer who demanded a fee of $1 million, with Montgomery to get 25 per cent. While in Greece in March, Montgomery supposedly solicited payoffs from Georgoulis's wife and Kalomiropoulos's brother. Alfantakis portrayed Montgomery as part of a conspiracy to extort money, and he charged Lloyd's with trying to implicate the two Greek officers in the *Salem* case in order to avoid paying insurance. For his part, Georgoulis maintained that a Liberian attorney asked him for $250,000 to cover bribes, and that the Liberian consul in Dakar had requested $2.5 million, claiming to know the son of then president Tolbert. He then lowered his demand to only $150,000.[28]

Alfantakis lauded Liberia's military government and portrayed the previous Tolbert administration as corrupt. He averred that the Bureau of Maritime Affairs was still staffed by remnants of the old regime, thereby attempting to taint it in that manner and discredit its efforts to have Georgoulis and Kalomiropoulos prosecuted. Allegedly, information about the Bureau's top officials was secured through private investigations and Montgomery in particular was made the prime target. Montgomery denied accepting any money or a plane ticket, but he did testify that his hotel bill in Piraeus and his taxi to the airport there were paid for by Alfantakis and Katsieris. He asserted that Alfantakis had threatened his life and that he had gone to his room to gather his belongings in preparation for departure from Greece. Upon returning to the lobby, he was informed by the hotel staff that the Greek attorneys had taken care of his bill. Then, as he arrived at the airport, the taxi driver told him that he too had already been paid.[29]

The Commission of Inquiry recommended to the Minister of Justice that prosecution of Georgoulis and Kalomiropoulos should proceed. It maintained that the extradition from Senegal had been carried out legally as the existence of an extradition treaty was irrelevant. States may extradite upon request even in the absence of such a treaty. Furthermore, the *Salem* was still registered in Liberia at the time of extradition as, contrary to Alfantakis's assertion, the provisional certificate of registry was not due to expire until June 2. The Commission agreed that indictment should have taken place earlier, but the statutory deadline had not yet been passed. It therefore called for formal indictment immediately. In regard to Doe's amnesty for prisoners, it determined that the names of Georgoulis and Kalomiropoulos had indeed been on the amnesty list, but not on a copy signed by President Doe. It concluded that their names had been included mistakenly and that the Liberian government had not intended to release them. The charges against Montgomery presented problems as no corroborating evidence was available. The Commission conceded, however, that Montgomery may have received some money and it could have been used to repatriate crewmen from Senegal to Greece. Montgomery's acceptance of funds was deemed 'irregular.'[30] Montgomery was soon suspended from his post, but later reinstated.

In June, President Doe made a surprise visit to the Monrovia prison and freed Georgoulis and Kalomiropoulos. The act was even shown on Liberian television. Doe apologized for their 'illegal detention,' indicated (despite the findings of the Commission of Inquiry) that there was insufficient evidence to prosecute, and claimed that the Liberian investigation had shown that they had done nothing wrong.[31] Georgoulis was then to boast at a press conference the following month: 'The fact that we were cleared of all charges proves our innocence.'[32] Doe's release of the pair could conceivably have been meant as an act of good will aimed at placating shippers angered by the tax increase. If so, it backfired, as the Liberian Shipowner's Council sent a letter of protest on June 26. A more pecuniary motivation has also been suggested, as there have been rumours of bribery. They cannot be substantiated, but it is clear that the Greek lawyers were prepared to spend any sum necessary to secure the release of the *Salem* officers.[33]

Commissioner of Maritime Affairs Gerald Cooper was in New York presenting a paper at a conference on maritime fraud. He heard about the release of Georgoulis and Kalomiropoulos on June 25 and declared that he was 'completely shocked' by Doe's decision. He asserted that his office was never consulted and he offered to provide documents to other countries willing to prosecute the pair. He also fired off a telex to Minister of Finance Perry Zulu indicating that he was 'dismayed' and that Liberia's respectability had been tarnished. Cooper warned that the registration of ships in Liberia could drop, and he asked if Georgoulis and Kalomiropoulos could be held for extradition to another country. It was already too late as they had departed. Cooper decided to resign his post but he kept his plans under wraps and continued to serve. He felt that he should first try to stabilize Liberia's shipping situation, and he also wanted to emphasize that his Bureau had played no role in the freeing of the two Greeks. Cooper hoped to prepare a final report on the *Salem* case to succeed the interim report completed in April, and he envisioned it as including an investigation into the circumstances of the June release. In August, the Liberian government decided that there would not be a final report. On September 12, Cooper announced his resignation.[34]

Heat Without Light

South Africa was faced with a serious problem after the *Salem* sank as Shell laid claim to the oil and then indicated on February 5 that it was taking legal action against the Strategic Fuel Fund.[35] An investigation into the affair was therefore undertaken by the SFF's director, Dr Dirk Mostert, and he managed to question the three major overt principals: Reidel, Soudan and Mitakis. His findings seem to have been somewhat contradictory, as he apparently cleared Soudan sufficiently to ask him to find more oil for delivery to South Africa, but parliamentary representatives of three opposition parties were informed that fraud had occurred.[36]

The South Africans possessed stolen oil, while Shell had suffered a full loss on the cargo as a result of its payment to Pontoil. Shell was already embarked on a course of seeking legal redress through the South African courts and officials in Pretoria had to head this off in order to maintain oil secrecy. A report prepared by the SFF, in explaining why an agreement with Shell was sought, asserted: 'During that period, it was not in the country's interests that the particular vulnerability of the RSA in obtaining crude oil be exposed.' Furthermore, the companies that were processing the *Salem*'s oil had to be protected from public revelations.[37] Consequently, discussions began in Amsterdam in early March. Shell rejected a compensation offer of $28 million, but $30.5 million was then accepted by both parties and a deal was announced on April 3. It was even reported in the South African periodical, the *Financial Mail*.[38] The $30.5 million was provided from the Equalization Fund, which was public money. Shell's loss had been $56.3 million, so it had settled for slightly more than half that sum. However, it retained the right to collect insurance payments for the cargo. Shell promised the SFF that any money recovered from the conspirators would be split evenly, and it dropped its legal action against the SFF.[39] Shell relinquished all rights to the oil, saying it could be refined 'without prejudice.'[40] According to Mostert, two innocent parties were splitting a loss.[41] Actually, South Africa had come out with less than 50 per cent and its innocence during negotiations with Soudan and Reidel was somewhat suspect.

Cabinet approval appears to have been given for the *Salem* settlement, and the South Africans have portrayed it as a favourable agreement, since Shell certainly had a valid claim.[42] In fact, they maintain that South Africa really gave away only $25.5 million rather than $30.5. This was due to the low purchase price paid to the perpetrators, as it was $5 million below the spot market and even more beneath Shell's cif price in the Pontoil transaction.[43] On the other hand, the SFF had surely paid twice for the same cargo and it had turned itself into a victim of cargo fraud.

Shell was unable to retrieve its lost oil. Tracing it would have been quite difficult as the buoy at which it was discharged is connected by pipeline to several tank farms, and part of the shipment had reportedly been mixed already with other crude. Some had even been refined. The *Salem*'s cargo was apparently distributed to at least three companies: Sasol, Mobil and Shell. Shell received its share (about 38 per cent) from a company that had owed it oil, so this amount was really paid for and was not a form of compensation. Rumours that Shell may have been given an import bonus by the South Africans, or may have been granted credits toward coal exports, are completely speculative and not buttressed by any available evidence. What is certain is that the stolen oil had disappeared and Shell had recouped a considerable part of its loss. This chapter in the *Salem* affair was over, as no court proceedings ever took place and the missing evidence flowed down into the petrol tanks of South African motorists.[44]

The SFF agreement with Shell resolved the financial aspects of the case. South Africa had no need to seek the retrieval of its loss as it was assured of receiving half of any funds recovered from the perpetrators by Shell.[45] Criminal sanctions against South African participants were another matter entirely, and it was here that considerable foot-dragging took place. The energy minister, Frederik Willem de Klerk, was not anxious to press an investigation as it was likely to reveal irregularities, or worse, in South Africa's oil procurement system. As the Transvaal leader of the ruling National Party, he was politically powerful and potentially a future prime minister. There was no need to rock the boat. By the summer of 1982, he had been succeeded in his energy post by Pietie T.C. du Plessis and the situation quickly changed. P.C. Swanepoel, an intelligence analyst in the prime minister's office, was chosen to investigate the *Salem* case. He was the former chief director of the National Intelligence Service, and Prime Minister Botha later referred to his investigation as one conducted by the NIS. Swanepoel initiated his effort on September 30 1982, which was more than thirty-two months after the *Salem* sank.[46] However, he did endeavour to be thorough. Swanepoel met with Reidel in the Netherlands, but he was unable to secure a copy of Reidel's file from the Dutch prosecutor D. Copper. He also questioned Mitakis and Georgoulis, but Locks refused to meet with him. In Britain, he spoke with insurance sleuth Robert Bishop and John Masters, but Scotland Yard was not helpful as it considered his investigation cosmetic and it resented the way Griggs had been received by the South Africans in February 1980. Swanepoel even met with Fred Soudan in Houston, where the *Salem*'s owner agreed to cede the hull insurance policy as a way of compensating South Africa for its financial loss. Soudan did send a copy, but it is unclear if legal cession was actually made. In any case, the South Africans never filed a hull claim. While in the United States, Swanepoel also queried Don Seaton.[47]

On November 18 1983, Swanepoel produced a report of more than three hundred pages based on his investigations through November 11.[48] It is a voluminous accumulation of evidence related to negotiations regarding the oil and the ship (with Shell and Pontoil being viewed rather suspiciously), but it includes only sparse analysis and excludes any investigation of South Africa's role. No information is provided on oil procurement methods, the decision-making structure of the SFF, or the agreement between the SFF and Shell. The issue of possible corruption is not broached, nor is it asked why the SFF never checked out the claims made by Soudan before arranging an oil deal with him. The Swanepoel report is an excellent compilation of relevant data, but it avoids areas that could embarrass South Africa. It is not a whitewash, just a failure to paint in Pretoria's colours at all.

Swanepoel's report was never released publicly, but the South African government decided in December 1983 that copies would be sent to assist foreign investigations. For that purpose, Minister of Mineral and Energy Affairs du Plessis granted a waiver of the Petroleum Products Act. Greece, the Netherlands, and the United States received copies on a confidential basis about February 1984, as did South Africa's Department of Mineral and Energy Affairs and an unnamed company in Switzerland. The Attorney-General of Cape province was also supplied with a copy to aid in his consideration of possible prosecutions. Progressive Federal Party opposition Member of Parliament John Malcomess said it was about time that something was being done and he called for release of the report in South Africa. He averred: 'We abhor secrecy provisions being used for coverup purposes. We also believe that these provisions create a fertile field for misappropriation and believe it is unwise to short-circuit Parliamentary control.'[49] The Swanepoel report was withheld from the public but the copy furnished to Greece was read in full into the *Salem* case court transcript in April 1985. Actually, maintaining the report's secrecy in South Africa did not hide very much from that country's citizens, for no bombshells were in it. Perhaps all that they would have learned about was the lax paperwork involved in oil procurement, including the acceptance of cargoes not accompanied by the original bills of lading.

Meanwhile, a conflict over secrecy in the *Salem* case raged in South Africa. As early as mid-1982, Malcomess had complained: 'It's public knowledge overseas as to who in South Africa paid the compensation and it's time that the taxpayers of this country were put fully in the picture by the Minister of Energy.'[50] Then, on February 16 1983, he raised the *Salem* issue in parliament and discussed the judgements presented by British courts in Shell's case against the cargo insurers. An uproar resulted as du Plessis attempted to ban publication of Malcomess's remarks. Normally, parliamentary comments could be cited in the press. In fact, many points were intentionally made within the confines of parliament as a means of circumventing censorship regulations. Du Plessis sought to challenge this procedure, but some newspapers refused to submit to government supplications and the attempt to tighten government controls resulted in failure. Freedom of the press, albeit of limited South African variety, prevailed as Malcomess's parliamentary statements unlocked areas previously closed to the public and led periodicals to discourse on the formerly taboo subject of the *Salem*.

Malcomess's revelations about the *Salem* also precipitated the Strategic Fuel Fund's memorandum to parliament in which it was claimed that South Africa was crude short and got involved with the *Salem* shipment as a temporary spot load measure until long-term contracts could be worked out with other suppliers. The chronology presented was somewhat strained, as the cancellation of a contract in December 1979 could not have led to the *Salem* affair; Soudan's initial agreement with the SFF was in October. Furthermore, the SFF had expected Soudan to deliver more than one load. The memorandum went on to declare: 'Secrecy of transactions is primarily aimed at protecting the RSA's crude oil suppliers and to retain their trust and in no way whatsoever to conceal information.'[51]

The SFF memorandum was submitted to parliament on March 9 1983 and a spirited debate on the *Salem* ensued. Malcomess had wanted a special parliamentary committee of inquiry to delve into the *Salem* affair. The government refused to establish it, but did agree to the parliamentary session and provided the Minister of Mineral and Energy Affairs, Pietie du Plessis, to respond to questions. Malcomess led the attack on the government's handling of the case, particularly its imposition of a veil of secrecy. He again referred to points raised in British court judgements and also read into the record sections of Barbara Conway's book, *The Piracy Business*, which contained a chapter on the *Salem*. Ironically, this study was available for sale in South Africa at a time when that country's press was gagged on the same subject. Malcomess asserted that details about the *Salem* were public knowledge abroad so South Africa's silence could not really be aimed at protecting its oil trade operations. The actions of South African officials were in fact being hidden from scrutiny, and the possible misuse of state funds had to be explored. Malcomess called for an investigation by the Advocate-General, and he additionally reiterated his demand for a select parliamentary committee. The latter would look into the recovery of funds, establish stricter legislative control over taxpayers' money, and determine the best means for preventing a similar occurrence. The opposition MP fumed: 'We are sold stolen goods which costs the public $30.5 million and we cannot even ask the police to investigate. Almost more than anything else this fact makes me smell a very large rat.'[52] Malcomess exaggerated somewhat as the Swanepoel investigation was then underway. However, he was surely correct that the government wanted to keep a tight lid on the affair. The Advocate-General was not asked to examine the financial transactions, and a parliamentary committee of inquiry was not formed. The gist of du Plessis' response was that oil secrecy had to be maintained. Although external reportage often included incorrect information, it was not in South Africa's interest to disclose the real facts. Discretion about Pretoria's oil vulnerability was a concern, but confidentiality was needed primarily to protect suppliers and shipowners.[53]

Controversy over South Africa's oil secrecy subsided, only to be renewed at fever pitch during the spring of 1984. In April, Progressive Federal Party leader Frederik van Zyl Slabbert forwarded to President Botha a dossier containing materials relevant to South Africa's oil trade. It included allegations of extensive mismanagement, and van Zyl Slabbert claimed that the charges had been given to him 'privately and anonymously.' He added: 'They were of an extremely serious nature and appeared to come from an authentic source.'[54] In the dossier were accusations that public money had been handled irregularly, and that more than $300 million had been expended over the oil import contract prices (excluding the amounts provided from the Equalization Fund). Five government or quasi-government officials were cited for possible personal aggrandizement from oil deals, allegedly including a former leading official of the SFF.[55]

The van Zyl Slabbert file concentrated on South Africa's oil deals with three prominent oil traders. The *Salem* case was not the prime focus, but the PFP leader's covering memorandum to

Botha stated: 'We also know that with regard to the *Salem* affair, the SFF itself did not lay a complaint with the Police or any other body to investigate the matter, nor have they done so to date despite the magnitude of the sum of money they lost.'[56]

Frederik van Zyl Slabbert called for two separate investigations: one by the Advocate-General to examine personal corruption, and the other by a select parliamentary committee to look into the incompetent expenditure of public funds. Botha agreed to send the dossier to the Advocate-General but he rejected the request for a special committee as it was deemend inconsistent with provisions of the Advocate-General Act. Botha maintained that the Advocate-General's report on the matter would be submitted to parliament; if the report was classified as confidential, only a select committee would consider it.[57]

Advocate-General Piet van der Walt's June 27 report (P.C. Swanepoel had given his full-time assistance to this investigation) cleared oil officials of corruption or overpayment. It also indicated, as the parliamentary opposition had complained previously, that the transactions of the Strategic Fuel Fund were not subject to review by the Auditor-General. No illegality was found, but the three traders emphasized in the allegations were not interviewed, nor was the SFF official. In an apparent contradiction, the report did declare that some South Africans may have been 'improperly enriched' as a result of the *Salem* affair.[58]

Dr Dirk Mostert had been the SFF's director when the *Salem* contract had been drawn up and, by the summer of 1984, he was serving as the senior general manager of Sasol and had no affiliation with the SFF. Claiming that oil transactions no longer had to be kept so secret, he averred that 'the *Salem* episode can now be made an open book.'[59] At an August seminar on 'The Prevention and Control of Maritime Fraud,' sponsored by the Johannesburg Chamber of Commerce, he asserted that South Africa was not the intended victim of the *Salem* fraud and that it had lost less than the $30.5 million paid to Shell, as it had purchased the oil at a favourable price. He discussed some of the terms of the Shell agreement and maintained that the conspirators were attempting to defraud the insurers. The chance arrival of the *British Trident*, and South Africa's announcement that the cargo had been discharged in Durban, then thwarted this plan. Mostert denied that South Africa had financed the purchase of the *Salem*. This was technically correct as the private Mercabank, not the SFF, had provided the letter of credit. However, the SFF had certainly agreed to guarantee its extension by promising to reimburse Mercabank out of the payment for the cargo. According to Mostert, the SFF extended no funds until the oil was delivered. This is indeed an accurate assessment, but the SFF's role in enabling Soudan to secure financing was much more crucial than Mostert would admit.[60] South Africa had gone public with the case, but it was unprepared to accept any responsibility.

On May 3 1985, the Attorney-General of Cape province announced that there would be no *Salem* prosecutions as no crimes had been committed by South African citizens. John Malcomess reacted by labelling South Africa 'the biggest losers' and he charged that oil secrecy laws were being used by the government to conceal 'at best negligence and at worst corruption.' Referring to the ruling National Party, he declared: 'I contend that the *Salem* affair was a prime example of abusing secrecy for reasons unconnected with the security of South Africa, but had every connection with the interests of the NP.'[61] Nevertheless, the case had been officially closed, so the *Salem* affair, like the vessel itself, had been laid to rest.

Salem investigations proliferated, but three countries that should have led the legal charge were notably slow to act. The perpetrators were nationals of Greece, the Netherlands and the United States but none of these states moved with alacrity, most likely since no financial loss had been incurred in their jurisdictions. The Piraeus public prosecutor began his investigation about September 1980, but there was a delay of more than four years before any defendants faced charges in court. In the Netherlands, Reidel was arrested in March 1981 but his trial did not start until 1986. The American case was more complex as an investigation of Soudan's tax payments was initiated early in 1980, and he was audited in August. Reports about the *Salem* affair had alerted the Internal Revenue Service, as did Soudan's outright purchase of a new home. However, no significant steps were taken by the Department of Justice regarding Soudan's role in the *Salem* conspiracy until the spring of 1982 when a representative of British insurance interests travelled to the United States to encourage prompt action. He conferred with federal prosecutors in both Houston and Washington, arguing that measures had to be taken against maritime fraudsters as

British insurers operating through Lloyd's of London were bearing the brunt. In May 1984, Soudan was arrested and he was brought to trial the following year.

Barristers at work

■ No legal contest developed over the *Salem*'s hull insurance as no claim was ever filed. Such was not the case in regard to the cargo insurance, as Shell demanded compensation for its lost oil. It had already recovered $30.5 million from the Strategic Fuel Fund, but was still out $25.8 million. Pressing its suit against Soudan was a hopeless proposition, as he had nowhere near that amount of money to his name. Shell therefore sought to collect on its insurance policy, which had originally been placed by Pontoil with underwriters in London.

Oil owned by Shell had clearly been stolen, and a small quantity had been lost at sea when the *Salem* went down off Senegal. Although Shell did not receive documents from Pontoil until after the sinking, its title to the oil was unquestioned and it definitely had the legal standing to seek payment from the insurers.[1] This produced the case of *Shell International Petroleum Company Ltd. v. Caryl Antony Gibbs*, more commonly referred to as *Shell v. Gibbs*. Portions of the *Salem*'s cargo insurance had actually been provided by sixty-nine syndicates and twenty-nine insurance companies but the insurers were collectively represented by one of their number, Gibbs.[2] He had assumed responsibility for upholding their position in the litigation as he had acted on behalf of the leading underwriting syndicate. The facts were not in dispute as the case of *Shell v. Gibbs* revolved solely around legal interpretations of the cargo insurance policy.

Opening Round

The case got underway on February 23 1981 at London's Commercial Court, Queen's Bench Division. Presiding was

Mr Justice Mustill and at stake was the fate of Shell's $56.3 million claim. At first, the insurers argued that the *Salem*'s voyage was not covered by the policy. It applied to a trip from Mina al-Ahmadi to Italy, but the conspiracy began even before the oil was pumped aboard and the intended destination was South Africa. The tanker therefore headed for Durban right from the start, and never started along its insured route. Shell countered with the claim that a conspiracy did exist, but it incorporated options alternative to the diversion to South Africa hypothesis. The ship could have been scuttled in an effort to collect on the hull insurance, the oil could have been marketed in Europe, or the ship could have been sold (leaving Mercabank in the lurch).[3] The defendants then withdrew their contention that the voyage was not covered by the policy, and they easily conceded that Shell's intention to deliver the oil to France presented no legal impediment despite the fact that Pontoil had been insured for a journey to Italy. The case therefore hinged upon the nature and circumstances of Shell's loss.

Mr Justice Mustill ruled on April 9 that Shell's entire loss was covered, as a 'taking at sea' had occurred when the ship left its course for Europe and cruised toward Durban. Up until this point, the shipowner had acted in Shell's interest. Therefore, the 'taking' had not been carried out in Kuwait when the tanker was loaded. In any case, that would not have been 'at sea' as the ship was in the port of Mina al-Ahmadi. The diversion to Durban was the key, even though the disposition of the cargo took place on land somewhat later. Mustill J. also asserted that Shell was entitled to recover its entire amount whether there had been one loss or two separate losses. It was really immaterial as the oil company was covered in the former situation under the 'taking at sea' clause; if the oil lost with the vessel was considered to be legally distinct from the oil delivered to Durban, it would be treated as an insurable 'peril of the sea.'[4]

One complication evident in the *Salem* case was that Fred Soudan, owner of the tanker, was party to the conspiracy. Mustill J. citing the *Mandarin Star* precedent of 1969, decided that the 'taking at sea' interpretation still applied. The *Mandarin Star* ruling had not greatly influenced the London insurance market in the past, as the policy in question had been issued in Japan. However, the judge's reliance on this British judicial precedent focused renewed attention on a serious problem and led to considerable controversy.

Shell had won its case, and stood to receive the full insurance coverage minus the sum already recovered from the South Africans. Of course, the underwriters sought another round in court.

Reversal

Lords Denning, Kerr and May of the Court of Appeal unanimously ruled on February 12 1982 that the bulk of Shell's loss was not retrievable under the insurance policy. A more expensive 'all-risks' policy would have covered theft by the shipowner, but Shell's did not. The Appeal judges differed sharply with Mustill's 'taking at sea' argument, maintaining that if a 'taking' did take place, it was in port. They therefore sustained Gibbs's contention, but differed among themselves as to whether there could have been a 'taking' at Mina al-Ahmadi. Lord Denning believed that this was possible, while Lord Justices Kerr and May disagreed and depicted the *Salem*'s loading as having occurred in a legal fashion irrespective of the intention of the perpetrators. The three judges concurred that 'a taking' may have been carried out in the port of Durban, but Shell was not covered since this was not 'at sea.'[5]

They also challenged Mustill's diversion to Durban scenario, arguing that the *Salem* may have altered its insured course, but not its intended course. The shipowner and master had planned to go to South Africa and did not act contrary to Shell's interests until the oil was discharged. This did not occur 'at sea' so there could not have been a 'taking at sea.' In addition, there had been no change in the possession of the cargo when the tanker changed course. Mr Justice Mustill had said that a change in the character of possession determined a 'taking at sea,' but the Court of Appeal judges determined that actual possession must be changed. Lord Justice Kerr claimed that the 'taking at sea' issue did not really pertain to Shell's loss even if it had been applicable as the loss was caused by the unloading in Durban and the subsequent scuttling.[6]

The Court of Appeal judgement ran counter to the *Mandarin Star* ruling, which was especially noteworthy as Lord Denning had joined in the court's decision thirteen years earlier. It was now established that the 'taking at sea' clause did not apply in instances where the shipowner or cargo owner participated in theft. The oil delivered to South Africa was therefore not 'taken at sea,' but what about the nearly sixteen thousand tons that were lost in the Atlantic? The judges agreed that the cargo had been lost in two stages, and the second stage had indeed been 'at sea.' Shell should thus receive insurance compensation for that amount as its loss was covered as a 'peril of the sea.'

The court considered many possible interpretations other than the 'taking at sea' approach; it ruled against Shell on all of them. 'Barratry' pertains to acts committed by the master or crew contrary to the interests of the shipowner, but it was deemed non-germane as Soudan was involved in the conspiracy. He could not have defrauded himself. Mustill had reached the same conclusion at the original court hearing as a theft by the carrier is not a normal peril covered by cargo insurance. Shell should have been more careful when it placed its oil in the hands of Soudan, the Shipomex bareboat charterers, and their appointed crew. According to a legal columnist for a shipping publication: 'The underwriters' argument was that insuring against the actions of crooks was an entirely different matter from insuring against the hiring of crooks.'[7] 'Piracy' was ruled out as no force was used and the shipowner and master were participants. Insurance against 'persons acting maliciously' was not applicable as the aim was theft rather than malice toward Shell, while decisions on 'other perils, losses and misfortunes' were dependent upon an affirmative interpretation of the 'taking at sea' issue.[8]

The cargo insurers had been successful in their appeal. They were still accountable for Shell's loss of oil in the sinking tanker, but were no longer required to compensate for the more substantial loss incurred in Durban. Shell had gone down to defeat, and insult was added to injury (although the obligation was standard on the part of the losing party) when the court required it to pay $73,600 for Gibbs's appeal! It was also ordered to pay $184,000, which amounted to half the court costs.

Final Verdict

Shell appealed against this judicial reversal, and Gibbs filed a cross-appeal regarding its obligation to cover the loss off

Senegal. The House of Lords then served as the highest legal arbiter in this matter and the case was brought before Lords Brandon, Brightman, Diplock, Roskill and Scarman. Lord Roskill's judgement, supported by the other four lords, was rendered on February 17 1983. It dismissed the appeal and cross-appeal, thereby sustaining the judgement of the Court of Appeal. All of the basic arguments of that court were considered justified. Shell was unable to make any headway with its claim that the *Mandarin Star* precedent had to be upheld, even if it had been wrongly decided in 1969. Shell maintained that it was influenced by that judgement and thought that it was applicable to its insurance policy at the time of receipt. Gibbs failed to sway the lords with its assertion that all of the oil had been lost upon loading in Kuwait so the quantity aboard the *Salem* when it sank could not have been lost as a 'peril of the sea.' Lord Roskill agreed that cargo fraud led to the loss, but it was not the proximate cause. Scuttling was and Shell was entitled to recovery on that basis as it was a 'peril of the sea.' Gibbs had been faced with the difficult burden of proving that the loss was not a 'peril of the sea', as the law did not require Shell to prove that it was or that the ship had been scuttled.[9]

Shell only received a little more than $4.5 million in insurance based on the *Shell v. Gibbs* judgement, plus another $5.2 million from an unrelated policy on the same cargo. It basically lost the case, even though its cargo was surely lost. The underwriters had won on technical, though valid and lawful, grounds and this led to some loss of respectability on their part. They had failed to pay off a reputable company, which had for years spent a huge sum on insurance premiums, in a case where there was no cause to suspect any collusion by Shell with the *Salem* fraudsters. Shell was thus depicted by a duo of maritime fraud experts as an 'innocent cargo-owner' which bought oil from an honest supplier, Pontoil. Its inability to acquire full compensation for its loss was adjudged a 'sorrowful example.'[10]

The *Shell v. Gibbs* case presented no jurisdictional problem as the cargo insurance had all been placed in Britain. It resolved the commercial aspects of the *Salem* affair, but the issue of criminal prosecution remained to be considered.

Days in Court

■ The legal process moved lethargically but the three main *Salem* perpetrators eventually were brought to trial, as were numerous other figures connected to the case. Differing jurisdictions and codes of law produced great diversity in the charges filed, and the diligence and competence of prosecutors also contributed substantially to the varying degrees of punishment (or lack of it) meted out to the defendants. Justice was not quite blind, but at least an effort was made to apply legal norms to those participating in international maritime fraud. Fred Soudan, perhaps undeservedly, received the longest sentence of all. Several important Greek defendants, who managed to stay safely in the background, were not convicted. The wheels of justice ground slowly, if not quite surely, as the *Salem* affair moved toward its final judgement.

Soft-pedalling in Rotterdam

Dutch authorities took their time in investigating the involvement of Anton Reidel. An arrest warrant had been issued in London in August 1980 and a report from Scotland Yard was then awaited as it could provide some useful evidence. It was received in February 1981, leading to Reidel's detention on March 6. The commodities trader was then held for eighty days, as the law stipulated that a person could be imprisoned for no more than one hundred days while awaiting trial. It was obvious that no trial would take place that quickly; in fact, preparations took five years!

James Shorrock, who had helped arrange the introduction to the Strategic Fuel Fund, was questioned in the Netherlands in 1981. South African investigator P.C. Swanepoel conferred with the prosecutor, D. Copper, in 1982 but there was little collaboration as the Dutch were unwilling to turn over a copy of Reidel's file. In 1983, two Dutch policemen were dispatched to the United States to get testimony from Soudan. Not only was the Rotterdam investigation carried out at a snail's pace, it was also riddled with procedural errors. Statements were given by Shorrock and Soudan, but they were later ruled invalid as defence counsel had not been given the right to be present during interrogation. No statement at all was solicited from Swanepoel, and it appears that his important status as the former director of the National Intelligence Service was not duly recognized by the prosecutor's office. The policemen who visited Soudan had also acted rather irregularly. They permitted themselves to be hosted by Soudan and relations apparently got so chummy that they were offered Mercedes Benz automobiles and 'a few days of fun' (apparently with gambling and women included) in New York and Atlantic City.[1]

The defence successfully delayed prosecution by insisting on the need for evidence from South Africa and from Georgoulis in Greece. It claimed that Swanepoel's investigation would help clear Reidel, and the South African report was therefore awaited up to its eventual receipt by the prosecution (the defence attorney was presented with a copy) early in 1984. Georgoulis was questioned in Greece late in 1983, but the prosecutor declared that his testimony was perjured. The defence wanted him to give a statement in the Netherlands, and it maintained that Georgoulis would be agreeable to this arrangement. Locating the elusive master of the *Salem* presented a complication, but his arrest by Greek authorities in February 1984 then provided some hope that he would appear in Rotterdam. At this stage, Mr Copper strangely declared that perjury charges could be filed against Georgoulis, but it would be very difficult to prosecute Reidel. Adding to the legalistic mayhem was Georgoulis' rapid release and the inability of the Dutch prosecutor to find him.[2]

Reidel asserted that his role in the *Salem* affair was minor and he therefore appealed against his indictment. In October 1984, a court in Rotterdam dropped five charges related to embezzlement, theft, and dealing in stolen goods but sustained three charges involving falsification of documents and swind-ling. Reidel then went to the Supreme Court in the Hague to seek further redress, a crucial mistake on his part. Not only were the three charges again sustained in a December 1985 judgement but a fourth was added on theft of oil! Once Reidel raised procedural objections regarding the three charges, the court was entitled to reexamine all of the original charges. It thus had the right to reintroduce any of the charges previously dropped by the appeals court in Rotterdam.[3]

In April 1985, Reidel had appeared as a defence witness at the trial of Soudan. This act probably served his cause, as unwillingness to present testimony may have had a negative effect on attitudes in the Netherlands. Finally, on February 5 1986, Reidel's own trial opened in Rotterdam before three judges, but no jury. Eleven hours of proceedings took place in one day. The prosecution presented its usual brief report and requested a three-year sentence. A six-year term was possible but leniency was recommended as Reidel was not known to have had prior convictions. There were actually thirteen charges, but nine of them were the same as the first four, albeit in more limited form. For example, misappropriation was the fallback charge for theft. The quartet of major charges were (1) falsifica-tion: Reidel was accused of signing a document indicating that he owned the oil (scratching out Pontoil's name from the bill of lading and signing on behalf of Oxford Shipping were also alleged at the trial); (2) swindling, as he was charged with using the document to mislead officials of the SFF; (3) persuading the SFF to accept a falsified document and (4) oil theft.[4]

The defence had prepared well for its day in court and introduced a fifty-three page document countering the charges. However, its attempt to have some charges dismissed was unsuccessful. It argued that the Netherlands didn't have jurisdiction as Reidel's firm, Beets Trading, was registered in Switzerland. It also questioned the validity of charges related to a broader conspiracy, as others had not been indicted.[5] The defence also failed to secure an adjournment so that Soudan and Shorrock could be sought as witnesses.[6] Attempting to subpoena Soudan would surely have consumed a considerable amount of time as he was already in gaol serving his sentence.

Reidel was questioned carefully by the panel of judges who were trying to determine if he was the 'mastermind' of the plot, as the prosecution had maintained. Reidel responded in a shrewd and calculating manner, appearing generally cooperative but yet careful to avoid self-incrimination. He admitted to serving as the disburser of the *Salem* funds, emerging with $4.2 million for himself. The issue of tax payments was not pertinent as Beets Trading had received the money and was subject to Swiss tax laws. In any case Reidel had earlier claimed that Beets had paid all taxes due to Switzerland.[7]

The testimony hinged around three basic documents. Of least concern was one signed by Reidel acting for Oxford Shipping. Reidel was not known to have been a legal agent for Oxford but he readily accepted responsibility for his signature with the explanation that he was present when the document had to be signed and Soudan, without warning, said he was appointed vice-president of Oxford. An hour later, after affixing his signature, he was fired. In fact, Soudan had authorized Reidel to act on behalf of American Polamax at the ship sale closing in London and at the port of Dubai, and this entitled him to represent Oxford as well.[8]

The more crucial documents were the bill of lading and the statement affirming that Beets Trading owned the oil. Both were pertinent to Reidel's December 19 1979 transaction with the SFF and there seems to have been some confusion in the court as to which item was being discussed at a given time. The prosecution argued that Reidel had fraudulently altered the bill of lading so he could then affirm ownership of the oil. By doing this, he was in fact demonstrating that the oil had been stolen. Reidel admitted that he had defaced the bill of lading and had claimed the oil belonged to Beets Trading. However, he asserted that he had presented what he believed to be the original bill of lading provided by Mitakis (although it had actually been sent to Pontoil and forwarded to Shell) and this entitled him to declare ownership of the oil. Reidel additionally indicated that altering the bill of lading was common practice in South Africa in order to conceal the identity of the supplier. He proclaimed that SFF officials had even asked Beets to serve as middleman in the transaction for that very purpose. As for the statement of ownership, Reidel said that it was drawn up by the SFF, not signed by its executives, and meant only for internal use. It was not an official document. As a matter of law in the Netherlands, it is not a criminal offence to prepare a document with false information unless it is used to mislead others. If the SFF was aware that Reidel didn't own the oil, and if the document was not presented in an effort to deceive any third party (which it wasn't), then Reidel could not be criminally liable. Leading officers of the SFF had not given statements on this matter to the Dutch prosecutor so the point of law was left hanging.[9]

After a hectic and lengthy day of legal parrying, the court adjourned to consider its verdict. On February 19, it was announced that a decision could not be rendered as further investigation along several legal avenues was required. Were South African authorities planning to press charges against Reidel? Were the charges in the Dutch indictment also criminal charges under South African law? If not, Reidel could not be held criminally liable in the Netherlands. Was Reidel convicted of cigarette smuggling in Naples, Italy? He had been rather vague when questioned on this matter and it was extremely pertinent to the issue of whether he should receive leniency as a first-time offender. Swanepoel had quaintly indicated in his report that Reidel sold cigarettes 'not always, it seems, with the knowledge or consent of the governments concerned.' Were SFF officials misled by Reidel? The court wanted more information from the South African government, and it sought Fanie Naude and Jan Bredenkamp as witnesses. It also sought statements from James Shorrock and P.C. Swanepoel. The court was expected to resume its deliberations in three months.[10]

The South Africans were unwilling to cooperate with the Dutch investigation. Swanepoel had not been assisted by the Rotterdam prosecutor more than three years previously, and the Klaas de Jonge affair was a thorn in the side of cordial bi-lateral relations. A Dutchman, he had been suspected by the South Africans of supplying arms and ammunition to the outlawed African National Congress. While in police custody, he escaped in July 1985 and entered the embassy of the Netherlands in Pretoria. He was then seized by the South Africans, but returned to Dutch custody eight days later after a strong protest from the embassy. The Dutch then granted him refuge and refused to return him to face charges. Passions over the de Jonge affair had not subsided and made the South African government even less amenable to furnishing witnesses for the Dutch court. Little could therefore be done as there was no Netherlands-South Africa treaty regarding the provision of witnesses.[11]

South Africa would not grant permission to question Naude and it claimed that Swanepoel was retired and couldn't be presented by the government. Shorrock could not be found. He no longer lived in South Africa, and had actually resided in the Netherlands for several years following the *Salem*'s sinking. Bredenkamp was in London serving as an officer of a West German company reportedly active in supplying oil to South Africa. He held joint South African and Dutch citizenships and could be prosecuted in South Africa for violating its oil secrecy laws should he reveal too much to Dutch investigators. Bredenkamp could not be extradited to the Netherlands as a witness and he indicated that he would only give a statement in South Africa and with the approval of Dirk Mostert, who had headed the SFF during the *Salem* negotiations. Of course, South Africa had no interest in having him queried as he was a storehouse of information on oil procurement and sanctions busting (including the practices in Rhodesia before it became Zimbabwe). The investigating magistrate in the Reidel case was in contact with Bredenkamp but she could not manage to secure him as a witness.[12]

The court was stymied and was not reconvened in May as planned. Instead, the prosecutor was given three more months to gather evidence. A reversal of roles was therefore taking place as the defence protested the repeated delays and called for a speedy acquittal. New information could only be damaging as the prosecution case presented in court was fairly weak. When the prosecutor was still not ready to proceed in August, the defence asked for a verdict within three weeks. Footdragging continued until February 25 1987 when Reidel's request for a rapid judgement was then rejected and his case postponed at least another six months. Due to mishandling of the prosecution, it appears that Reidel may be acquitted on all counts. If convicted, it may only be on the fourth, or lesser, charge of theft. If Reidel is found guilty on any charge, the Dutch case should still roll merrily along as he can petition the appellate court and, later, the Supreme Court. If all charges are dismissed, he can seek financial compensation for the days spent in gaol.[13]

The prosecution acted rather clumsily in the Netherlands and Reidel is unlikely to receive any substantial penalty. Witnesses were questioned improperly without the presence of defence counsel, no statement was taken from Swanepoel, and Shorrock was not sought as a witness when he was within Dutch jurisdiction. There was also some sloppy homework as the vagaries of South African law were not examined and it was not clarified whether Reidel had a prior conviction in Naples.

Mostert was never contacted to give testimony, while the behaviour of the two policemen in the United States made the prosecutors reluctant to have them testify about what they learned from Soudan.[14] Admittedly, the prosecution was confronted with some obstacles. South Africa was obstructive, and the sinking of the *Salem* was outside Dutch jurisdiction. Income tax charges were uncommon in the Netherlands, but could not even be considered as Beets Trading was a Swiss company. Furthermore, Reidel had to be tried under the fraud laws as they existed at the time of his alleged offences, even though they had been significantly strengthened since. Nevertheless, the defence outshone the prosecution and its competence was clearly rewarded.

Perambulations in Piraeus

The Greek investigators sought assistance from Scotland Yard as a British arrest warrant had been issued for Georgoulis. In January 1981, officers of the maritime police visited London and the Scotland Yard report on the *Salem* case was then provided. Despite this evidence, the Ministry of Justice was still uncertain whether Greece should prosecute its own nationals. It questioned Athens's jurisdiction over alleged crimes committed outside of Greek territorial waters and suggested that Liberia could possibly serve as the most appropriate jurisdiction.[15] However, the Piraeus public prosecutor then concluded that there were grounds for prosecution in Greece and charges were filed in September 1981 against Georgoulis, Mitakis, Annivas and Kalomiropoulos. Outside economic interests had pressed for such action as many shippers and insurers had accused Greece of reluctance to prosecute cases of maritime fraud, particularly in regard to the *Salem* affair. Especially noteworthy was the March 12 petition from the International Maritime Bureau, backed by numerous insurers and brokers, to the Minister of Justice George Stamatis.[16]

Procedural delays plagued the *Salem* case. New Minister of Justice George-Alexander Mangakis said that such problems existed throughout the Greek judicial system, but a decision was reached to establish within a year a maritime court in Piraeus which would hear fraud cases. Enabling legislation was drawn but a court order led to the abandonment of the plan as it had included the acceptance at trials of untranslated documents in foreign languages.[17] However, an important change in the law was effected in March 1984. It stipulated that a trial could proceed even though some of the accused were not present in court, thus rendering it more difficult for the defence to create delays.

Before a trial could take place, the issue of double jeopardy had to be considered. Georgoulis and Kalomiropoulos claimed that they had already been acquitted in Liberia, and an October 10 1982 statement issued by a Monrovia court affirmed that they had been found 'not guilty'. However, other evidence indicated that they had never been tried and that Doe had released them as 'the above crimes had not taken place.' Liberian Minister of Justice Jenkins Scott maintained that the two officers had never been tried in Liberia and that documents asserting otherwise were a 'misrepresentation of facts.' Greek authorities then decided that prosecution should proceed as there was no double jeopardy.[18] Overall, the Liberians were helpful to the Greek prosecution as they wanted to compensate for the negative effects engendered by Doe's release of Georgoulis and Kalomiropoulos and improve their image in the shipping trade.

Twenty-five defendants were named in the Greek indictment. Thirteen had been aboard the *Salem*, including the master Georgoulis; seven were foreigners; and five were Greeks connected to the affair, such as Mitakis. Strangely, all Greek crewmen but one were indicted, the lone exception apparently being a third engineer named G. Moros. The non-Greeks listed were Fred Soudan, Anton Reidel, Wahib Attar, Hasso Osterkamp, Johannes Locks (identified as 'Bert Samuel Stein'), Johan Locks and Thomas Locks. The inclusion of three defendants named Locks must have been an error as Johannes and Thomas were probably the same person. In addition to Mitakis, the non-*Salem* Greeks named were Gregorios Makrygiorgios, Eleftherios Afentakis, Nikolaos (Nick) Makris and Panagiotis Daglas. Christos Hatzichristos, who had allegedly paid off the crew in Dakar, was not indicted. The crewmen were charged with simple complicity in the theft of the oil; the foreigners with embezzling the cargo, planning the scuttling and instigating an insurance fraud; Mitakis with direct complicity in

108

the theft, attempted insurance fraud and planning the scuttling; and the other four Greeks with being accessories to simple complicity.

According to the indictment. Makrygiorgios and Afentakis helped select the crew and to create the false name of 'Stein.' Afentakis was also accused of booking rooms in Geneva during the period November-December 1979 so that 'Stein' could meet with Mitakis. Daglas was cited for his role in Durban where he allegedly permitted the oil to be discharged once a signal from Mitakis had been received that the payment had been made. He also was named as the person who allegedly distributed Swiss francs to crew members so they would keep quiet about the discharging in South Africa. Makris allegedly went to Dar es Salaam, boarded the *Salem*, and assured the crew of their salaries plus extra money. This is highly unlikely as Makris was apparently being detained by Swiss authorities at the time on unrelated charges pertaining to a questionable letter of credit.[19] None of the numerous *Salem* investigations corroborated the Greek account on this matter.

Makrygiorgios, Makris and Afentakis were active in the Greek shipping industry. Makrygiorgios had apparently owned the *Brilliant* and *Alexandros K.*, and he was possibly linked to cargo diversion aboard the *Camelia*. Interestingly, a call to him seems to have been made from Shorrock's room at the Royal Hotel in Durban the same day the *Salem* arrived. Makris's name appeared on the February 2 1979 investigators' list of suspected participants in maritime fraud. On December 3 1979, he apparently was registered at the Rotary Hotel in Geneva, as was 'Bert Stein.'[20] Afentakis purportedly had connections to the *Betty*, which loaded steel in Italy and wood in Yugoslavia. It was supposedly bound for Jiddah, Saudi Arabia, but its cargo was sold in Lebanon.[21] All of these men were suspected of cigarette smuggling, and it appears that this activity brought them into contact with Reidel and the younger Locks. It has even been suggested that the name *Salem* derives from the cigarette brand. Georgoulis had served as master of Makrygiorgios's vessel the *Alexandros K.* (and then had become its part owner), and it should be added that his brother-in-law Annivas was somewhat more than a first mate. He had a master's license and was probably a shipowner as well. He was the acknowledged technological expert on the tanker and, according to the testimony of radioman Vassilios Evangelides, he was on duty when the alarm was raised off Senegal. Some believe that Annivas was really the person in charge aboard the *Salem*.[22]

Complications affected the course of justice as Georgoulis and Annivas were not in custody, and did not appear. Georgoulis had been arrested in February 1984, but released. He later charged that he and his family had been threatened with violence if he told the truth, and that members of the crew had been paid off to conceal information.[23] In fact, the crewmen did maintain a rather formidable united front as many were from the same village and some were relatives. By the time of the scheduled trial on January 9 1985, Mitakis had spent sixteen months in gaol, and Kalomiropoulos fourteen. Mitakis then claimed a heart problem, which set back proceedings four days. Once the court was finally in session, the case was postponed until March 20 as the defence emerged victorious with its contention that all documents had to be translated into Greek. The prosecution also wanted time to find out how far Senegal's territorial waters extended, whether any Senegalese laws had been violated, and whether Liberia had valid jurisdiction.[24] Upon reconvening, there were further difficulties. On one day, no room for the trial was available in the court building. Another day was lost as it was devoted to mourning for an assassinated public prosecutor. Then there was a brief delay so that the newly translated Swanepoel report could be read by interested parties.[25]

Eventually, a two-and-a-half week trial took place. A five-judge panel, headed by Haralambos Pampoukis, heard the case and only thirteen of the eighteen Greek defendants were present. None of the indicted foreigners appeared. An informal atmosphere prevailed as food was eaten during the proceedings, journalists mingled with lawyers and walked up to the front of the courtroom to hear better, and the defendants socialized with newsmen during breaks. Noises from the nearby port and market constantly drifted into the courtroom. Mitakis often held his head in his hands, and he seemed to be depressed and passive when not giving testimony. He said that he was appearing against the advice of his doctors, who feared that his heart was too weak to bear the strain. Kalomiropoulos wept while on the stand, and members of the crew accentuated the hard times they had presumably encountered since the *Salem*'s fateful voyage. They were trying to demonstrate that they had not become rich from payoffs, and this may indeed have been the case for some defendants, as the legal counsel they had retained was undistinguished. Mitakis later claimed that $1.5 million had been given to Afentakis for crew costs, and another $2,850,000 for that purpose was provided at the insistence of 'Stein.' However, the amount actually received by members of the crew remains unclear. It was surely a fact that the wife of Kalomiropoulos was earning money driving a taxi, while a seaman named George Gerakoulis maintained that he had become a door-to-door encyclopedia salesman. Mitakis too cited financial distress, asserting that one of the pair of houses he owned had been sold and the other mortgaged so he could pay his legal expenses. Certainly, Mitakis had two of Greece's most prominent attorneys: Alexander Lykourezos and Nikolaos Androulakis.[26]

The gist of the proceedings was that the defendants admitted the delivery of oil to South Africa, but they denied participation in scuttling. The defence argued that no cargo theft had taken place, as Shell knew the oil would be taken to Durban. The prosecution stressed Shell's innocence, citing Scotland Yard's report clearing both Shell and Pontoil. The defence request to have officials of Shell and Pontoil testify was rejected by the judicial panel.[27] Overall, the defence blamed foreigners for the *Salem* affair but little concrete evidence was presented against the non-Greek defendants in absentia.

On April 8, the verdict was announced. Mitakis was found guilty and his fourteen years of sentencing on three charges were combined into an eleven-year term. Kalomiropoulos got four years, second engineer Ioannis Mavros and third engineer George Theodossiu three apiece, and radioman Vassilios Evangelides received two years and two months. The prosecution agreed to the acquittal of all other Greeks. Five non-Greeks were sentenced to three years each. Osterkamp and Thomas Locks appear to have been acquitted, although it is possible that charges were dismissed against Locks once it was found out that only two gentlemen named Locks should have been cited in the indictment. None of the foreigners were within Greek jurisdiction, so none were ever imprisoned. However, Reidel did appeal against his conviction on the ground that no effort was made to have him appear in court: the trial in absentia was therefore invalid. Reidel was successful, his conviction was dropped, but he could still be brought to trial should he ever travel to Greece.[28]

Annivas and Georgoulis, as Greek citizens, could not be sentenced in absentia. Annivas eluded arrest, but Georgoulis was nabbed outside his home on October 5 1985. His trial was scheduled for January 31, but then postponed until February 12 as some witnesses were absent. At a pre-trial hearing, the defence complained that three of the five judges presiding over the case, including Pampoukis, had served at the earlier trial. The entire judicial panel then disqualified, itself, but a new panel dismissed the defence's objection and reinstated the original five judges. Georgoulis's trial then took only two days as most of the evidence against him had already been presented at the previous trial. Only his wife appeared as a defence witness. Georgoulis said that he didn't know the oil was delivered to South Africa illegally until after he arrived there. Also in Durban, he was given orders to scuttle the ship to conceal the cargo theft. Crew members were also apprised, paid off, and their assent secured. The *Salem*'s master was quickly convicted of cargo fraud and scuttling. His fourteen years of penalties were combined into a twelve-year term.[29]

Meanwhile, the effort by those Greeks convicted in 1985 to have their verdicts reversed on appeal was stalled as the court first wanted to conclude the Georgoulis trial. Once he was sentenced, his appeal was attached to theirs and a seven-judge panel was appointed to hear the case. Mitakis admitted that he received $20 million under the name 'Nicholas Trilizas,' but he denied prior knowledge of cargo fraud or scuttling. Georgoulis was more forthcoming as he may have hoped to have the charges reduced to a misdemeanour, which would have entailed a maximum term of five years. He described the scuttling, which was still denied by the *Salem* seamen, and he accused Makris of trying to bribe the crew not to reveal the scuttling by giving them forged checks. Georgoulis, accompanied by his entire family, was rather cheerful throughout the proceedings. Mitakis also appeared happier than at his earlier trial, but he had lost a considerable amount of weight in the meantime. On May 26, the judicial panel reduced the sentences of Mitakis to eight years, Georgoulis to seven, Kalomiropoulos to three, Theodossiu to two and a half years, and Mavros to two years and two months. Evangelides received no shortening of his term.[30] Mitakis and Georgoulis then took their case to the Supreme Court to seek further redress.

The Greek legal system eventually worked, but not without

having experienced some rather ludicrous incidents along the way. Three people named Locks were indicted, Georgoulis was not imprisoned pending trial, Makris was charged with an offence he probably could not have committed, and a confidential report supplied by South Africa was made public. It also appears that no effort was made to extradite the foreign defendants and the charges against them were in some instances farfetched, and even farcical. It was extremely unlikely that either Locks had anything to do with the scuttling, or that Attar was involved in attempted insurance fraud. None of the charges seem to have been pertinent to Osterkamp's role, but he was rightfully acquitted.

Overkill in Houston

Armed with investigatory reports from Scotland Yard and South Africa, the American prosecutors presented their case against Soudan to a federal grand jury. On May 24 1984, the owner of the *Salem* was indicted on twenty-two counts which could have led to 110 years in gaol plus a $93,000 fine. There were thirteen counts of wire fraud, three of perjury, two each of obstructing justice and filing false tax returns, and single counts related to the interstate transport of stolen property and making false statements. Soudan's forty-seven-year-old Syrian brother-in-law, Abdul Wahab al-Ghazou, was also indicted on three counts. He had been questioned about his role in hiding some of Soudan's proceeds in an effort to avoid taxes and his unsatisfactory responses had led to two counts of conspiracy to obstruct the tax authorities plus an added charge of making false statements to the grand jury. Soudan and al-Ghazou were promptly imprisoned and an arrest warrant was issued for James Shorrock, who had helped Soudan in South Africa. A British citizen living in the Netherlands, he had been indicted on three counts related to statements regarding his receipt of payment from Soudan. He was immediately arrested by Dutch authorities, extradited to the United States, and put in gaol.[31]

Next came an interesting round of plea bargaining. Soudan and the prosecution agreed that he would plead guilty to two counts of tax fraud and one each on conspiracy to obstruct justice and issuing a false statement, but he would continue to deny

knowledge that the oil was stolen or that the tanker was to be
scuttled. Soudan relinquished his rights to file for the hull
insurance and to claim funds in a frozen Swiss account, and
Shell, the Strategic Fuel Fund and the cargo insurers were
invited to seek restitution of more than $2 million. Soudan could
have been sentenced to eighteen years' imprisonment for the
counts on which he pleaded guilty, but the prosecutor accepted a
six-year term and a $26,000 fine. Al-Ghazou's attorney plea-
bargained his possible term down from five years to three, while
Shorrock fared best of all after pleading guilty to one count of
conspiracy to obstruct justice. Judge Carl O. Bue accepted the
Shorrock plea-bargain but, in a rather uncommon move, rejected
those of Soudan and al-Ghazou without explanation. Apparently, there was more to the Shorrock plea than was apparent in
the written agreement, as he became a prosecution witness. His
sentencing was to be imposed after the completion of his co-
defendants' trial, so an effective performance on his part was to
be anticipated.[32]

The jury was unaware of the two rejected plea-bargains when
the trial opened on January 8 1985 in Houston's Federal District
Court. Judge Bue presided, Randy Bellows and Brenda Gruss
were the prosecutors, and Bruce L. Locke and David Berg served
as defence attorneys for Soudan and al-Ghazou respectively.
James Shorrock was among the numerous witnesses testifying
for the prosecution, while Anton Reidel, with a promise of 'safe
passage' from the Department of Justice, appeared for the
defence. According to American legal practice, the defendant has
the option of taking the stand. Soudan did not do so and he
watched the proceedings quietly, with an air of dejection. He
was accompanied by a clergyman who was presumably present
to serve as a translator even though Soudan's English was
rather good.

The eleven-week trial illuminated the *Salem* affair in great
detail, but the most significant legal battle revolved around the
role of South African witnesses. Swanepoel, after receiving a
waiver from his government so that he could not be prosecuted
for violating oil secrecy laws, came to Texas to testify. However,
Naude, Bredenkamp and Mostert were not given such a waiver
and they therefore withdrew their offer to serve as witnesses. As
they were not physically present in the United States, they
could not be subpoened. These three men had been officials of
the Strategic Fuel Fund, and the defence therefore called for a

mistrial on the ground that those who were supposedly defrauded were not available to testify. It claimed that there was really no victim as the SFF had collaborated in acquiring oil illegally, and where there was no victim there was no fraud. David Berg declared: 'These people were the ones our government claims were defrauded. If they don't want to come and complain, it indicates to me that they were not defrauded by Soudan.'[33] The effort to secure a mistrial was unsuccessful and the proceedings continued without any testimony from the SFF.

Actually, the defence was largely responsible for the non-appearance of Naude, Bredenkamp and Mostert. The prosecution went to great lengths to assuage South African sensibilities over the matter as it realized that Pretoria would not provide the three officials if they were to be grilled about recent methods of oil procurement. According to a pre-trial statement by the prosecution: 'While South Africa's practices at the time of the *Salem* transactions may or may not be a relevant area of inquiry, the government will object to questions about current oil procurement practices as beyond the scope of cross-examination, irrelevant, and cumulative.... Since the government will in no way touch upon the subject of South Africa's oil procurement practices in the five-year period from 1980 to the present, any questions about current oil procurement plainly exceed the scope of cross-examination and should be proscribed.'[34] Such ground rules may have encouraged South Africa's cooperation but the defence felt hamstrung by these provisions as it wanted to reveal Pretoria's 'twilight world.' If it could be demonstrated that South Africa frequently engaged in illegal oil practices and intentionally overlooked misrepresentations made by suppliers, then it would be much easier to prove that no fraud had taken place. In other words, the SFF should have known or suspected that it was receiving stolen oil. The defence was unwilling to limit its legitimate courtroom prerogatives, leading a South African magazine to conclude: 'In view of the judiciary's independence and the fact that the defence would not be bound by undertakings given by the American state, adequate undertakings could not be obtained. After consulting American and London lawyers, the SFF witnesses, in consultation with the SA government, decided that it was inadvisable to testify in Houston, but reiterated their willingness to give evidence on commission in SA. Neither the prosecutor nor the defence requested that evidence be taken on commission.'[35]

115

The prosecution presented an overwhelming barrage of evidence, while the defence had few exhibits of its own and made little leeway in discrediting the prosecution's case. Defence counsel must have realized its weak position as, in his final argument, Locke said that Soudan admitted his guilt regarding tax evasion and lying under oath about payments to South African brokers.[36] On March 26 1985, the jury found Soudan guilty on seventeen of the twenty-two counts. He was acquitted on five counts of wire fraud as they had occurred prior to his agreement with the SFF. Al-Ghazou was convicted on all three counts. On April 29, Judge Bue sentenced Soudan to thirty-five years (but no fine), and al-Ghazou to five years. Shorrock was sentenced to time already served, plus five years of probation. Soudan was ordered to forfeit the funds in three bank accounts (two in Switzerland and one in the Bahamas), the money to be used to compensate Shell and the cargo insurance underwriters in the ratio of five to one. Restitution up to a total of $4.25 million was eventually to be paid should additional funds from the fraud be recovered. Although Soudan was convicted of tax evasion, Judge Bue could not legally require him to recompense the Internal Revenue Service as a separate court action was required. There was no stipulation that Soudan pay for the cost of prosecution as Judge Bue preferred that all available funds should be earmarked for restitution.[37]

Soudan was to be eligible for parole after serving ten years, and al-Ghazou after completing one-third of his term. For both men, the eleven months already served were to be counted toward their sentences. Soudan appealed and his case was scheduled to be heard in New Orleans before the Fifth Circuit of the Federal Court of Appeals. Meanwhile, he was imprisoned with no right to bail.

Bellows and Gruss were extremely effective in gathering evidence, presenting it clearly, and assembling relevant witnesses. They successfully sought prosecution on a wide variety of charges, somewhat stretching the count regarding conspiracy to scuttle. There was no evidence indicating that Soudan was party to a scuttling plot, but he could still be charged as long as he was participating in a broader conspiracy and could reasonably anticipate that his co-conspirators would scuttle.[38] Bellows's opening statement also pressed the case very strongly. It is not considered to be evidence and the prosecutor is permitted some leeway in his remarks. Bellows surely used it when he claimed that Soudan had tried to mortgage the *Salem* the same day it sank; evidence presented later did not clearly establish the appropriate date. Similarly, Bellows maintained that the crew departed from the lifeboats 'in suits and ties,' but prosecution exhibits featuring statements by Captain Taylor and Chief Officer Martin of the *British Trident* indicated that they were dressed in the normal manner for seamen.[39] Once Soudan was convicted, Bellows still did not relent. He orchestrated a letter-writing campaign from prominent figures in legal and shipping circles apparently in order to convince Judge Bue, before passing sentence, that maritime fraud was a most serious matter demanding strict enforcement. Bellows's request for advice to the court on the importance of the *Salem* case to the maritime community brought a significant response. This procedure was legal and ethical as Judge Bue was informed that the letters had been solicited by the prosecutor.[40]

The defence performed poorly, as it didn't challenge the conspiracy to scuttle charge or try to show that Soudan was unaware of a plan to scuttle. Locke and Berg often questioned witnesses without properly anticipating the responses, and they failed to contest exaggerated allegations made in Bellows's opening statement. These allegations were surely not sufficiently prejudicial to warrant a mistrial, but there is an obligation on the part of the prosecutor to substantiate them during the trial with supportive evidence. The defence could have pointed this out, and the judge may then have instructed the jury that part of the prosecution's case was not proven. In addition, the defence aimlessly argued that insurers pressured the United States to prosecute Soudan so that he couldn't collect on a hull claim. Not only was evidence lacking on this point, but so was credulity. Prior to his indictment in May 1984, Soudan had already had more than four years to file an insurance claim and he had not done so.[41]

On December 15 1986, a three-judge panel affirmed Soudan's conviction and rejected his appeal on all grounds. One contention had been that Soudan was denied effective assistance of counsel as his lawyer, Bruce L. Locke, had an attorney-client relationship with a prosecution witness, James Shorrock. The court found that no such relationship had existed.[42] A second ground for appeal was that the jury should have been instructed that to find Soudan guilty, it would have had to believe that he knew the oil was stolen and that the tanker would be scuttled.

117

Otherwise, the offences discussed at the trial would have served to broaden the terms of the indictment. The judges ruled: 'The court's instruction guaranteed the jury did not return a guilty verdict on a theory which broadened the scheme outlined in the indictment. The jury had a basis upon which to find the defendant criminally culpable within the scope of the indictment. No constructive amendment or prejudicial variance is evident from the record.'[43] A third claim was that the admission of testimony regarding the use of *Salem* proceeds to pay for an abortion for Soudan's secretary had been irrelevant or prejudicial. The appellate court determined, however, that the disbursal of the proceeds had been a legitimate area of inquiry, as it was pertinent to Soudan's assertions about how the money was spent and the tax status of these funds. Lastly, the allegation that the prosecution had commented on Soudan's failure to testify was deemed incorrect. The judges maintained that there had been no such prejudicial remark, only a reference to the defence's failure to counter certain testimony.[44]

Judge Bue, who had not accepted Soudan's plea-bargain with the prosecution in 1984, had remained silent on his decision for nearly three years, as any explanation could have prejudiced Soudan's right to a fair trial and appeal. Once such an appeal failed, Judge Bue revealed: 'My reasons for rejecting the initial Soudan plea bargain were quite basic. It was highly disproportionate and narrowly focused and failed to address the magnitude of the crime committed.' If the Department of Justice had at first been somewhat too accommodating, it was soon spurred into decisive action. Judge Bue commented: 'The Government thereafter went all out to assemble proof on all of the issues as the record reflects.'[45]

Due to a zealous and effective prosecution and a lacklustre defence, Fred Soudan had emerged from the *Salem* legal wars with the strongest penalty. He may have been less culpable than others but he had been set up as a front man and he suffered the consequences.

Assessing the damage

■ The *Salem* affair will have a lasting impact on the shipping and insurance industries and, like the issue of the 'fifth man' in the British spy scandal, it will forever continue to haunt and provide new areas of inquiry. Various legal appeals should keep the case in the limelight for years to come, and any repetition of maritime fraud on such a vast scale is bound to produce comparisons with the *Salem*. While the full implications of the *Salem* affair may not yet be known, sufficient repercussions have already been felt, so that a preliminary overview should still be most instructive.

Plotting

One irony emerging from the 'fraud of the century' is that so much commotion and frenetic negotiating activity was engendered by a supply of oil that probably didn't exist. Brokers and traders were sent scurrying across several continents in the hope of making the deal of a lifetime, but there is no evidence that Mitakis or Reidel ever owned (or took steps to buy) the six cargoes of crude that lay at the heart of the financial argy bargy. Is it possible that there actually was such an oil supply? Perhaps the account about 'topping,' bareboat chartering, replacing discharged crude with seawater, and obtaining false certification of delivery was indeed the plan, and that there was originally no intent to steal a cargo? Maybe the need to deliver crude to South Africa in December rather than February disrupted earlier calculations, and the cargo that was to be loaded was not yet available? There are two problems with such an interpretation. Who was going to pay for the oil? The mass of communications related to the *Salem* affair does not reveal any mention of raising funds to purchase the crude, and no financing was apparently sought. Even if the oil had been 'topped,' it surely would not have been provided free of charge. Secondly, who had the oil if it had been gradually 'topped'? If the perpetrators had somehow managed to accumulate enough crude for a full load, this would have taken place in Saudi Arabia. Once they used Pontoil's cargo, whatever happened to the oil waiting at Ras Tanura? There is no indication that there was any disposal of such a presumably lucrative supply. If Shell or Pontoil had engaged in 'topping,' they would unnecessarily have been party to a complex conspiracy, for they could easily have sold the cargo on their own. There was no reason to peddle it through Mitakis and Reidel.

Many questions have been raised by Shell's role in the *Salem* affair. Shell was active in the South African oil industry in terms of securing imports and refining crude, and it was also supplying cargoes directly. As a result of its collaboration with South Africa, Shell was strongly criticized by anti-apartheid movements and its involvement in the *Salem* case was bound to arouse suspicions. Shell had considered chartering the *Salem*, had convinced Mitakis to drop the Kuwait exclusion, and had then backed out of a deal. Two weeks later, Shell reversed its position by buying Pontoil's cargo at a high price and it even agreed to pay for transport at a rate greater than it could have received from Oxford. Shell then participated in the discharge at the single buoy mooring, allegedly acquired part of the cargo, and then paid Pontoil in full even though the load aboard the *Salem* had not reached its intended destination, France. Shell then settled with the SFF for much less than the full value of its oil, withdrawing from an effort to secure redress through South African courts. To construct a conspiracy hypothesis, it could be argued that Shell plotted to supply its own refinery operations in South Africa, then got reimbursed by the SFF for oil that was supposedly stolen, and then planned to cash in again on the cargo insurance. In addition, it could be pointed out that Soudan may have obtained assistance from Shell, as he may have known about the voyage plans of the *Lima* and *Limatula* before informing the South Africans that his tanker would arrive as the *Lema*.

120

Efforts to implicate Shell are confronted by some stark realities. Shell notified the British courts that it was prepared to subtract the $30.5 million settlement with the SFF from a favourable judgement. There is also no evidence that any of the perpetrators ever communicated with Shell prior to the sinking, or that Shell emerged with any of the funds disbursed by Reidel. Shell was also cleared by investigations in Britain, the United States, the Netherlands and Greece. Most important of all is the fact that had Shell known its oil was already in South Africa, it would surely have attempted to collect payment before the *Salem* was scuttled.

The *Salem* conspiracy was so broad that there were numerous compartmentalized subplots and little grand design. Improvisation was often required, forcing careful calculations to go asunder. Seaton was both in and out of the escapade, the February delivery was moved up to December, a letter of credit had to be obtained from Mercabank, the *Paula* was replaced by the *Salem*, Kuwaiti oil was substituted for Saudi, and Pontoil's cargo came to be Shell's. Participants in the *Salem* plot often lacked important information known to others. Reidel may have been unaware of Soudan's first visit to South Africa, just as Soudan probably was ignorant of 'Stein's' identity and didn't realize that the crude offered by Reidel and Seaton was really the same oil. Both Reidel and Soudan may have been in the dark on Pontoil's sale of the cargo to Shell, and the knowledge of each pertaining to the planned scuttling is certainly up for conjecture. Mitakis may not have been cognizant of many of the arrangements with the SFF but, overall, he had a more complete grasp of the situation than either Reidel or Soudan as he handled the supply of oil, the chartering of the vessel to Pontoil, and the hiring of the crew. He also knew 'Stein' and was in contact with Makris and Afentakis. Mitakis may even have heard about Shell's transaction with Pontoil, as he was regularly in touch with the ship brokerage firm Genpe, and Genpe formed part of the communications chain of command relating to the *Salem*.

Fred Soudan got the oil contract with South Africa and financing for the tanker, while Don Seaton did not. Nevertheless, Soudan was rather amateurish in many ways. He didn't insist on a performance bond from Reidel, he bareboat chartered his tanker to the unknown 'Stein;' he trusted Reidel with the money, and at first, did not receive his full payment; he almost lost Oxford Shipping; and he spent too lavishly, attracting the attention of the US tax authorities. If he was not party to the scuttling plan, he vexingly had his major asset disappear beneath the sea. Soudan, as the owner of the *Salem*, also became the public point man after the scuttling as he had to suffer the slings and arrows of the media and investigatory agencies. Why the SFF selected this man's offer of crude out of its plethora of alternatives may forever remain a mystery due to South Africa's blanket of secrecy.

Soudan experienced some bad luck that was beyond his control. His plea-bargain was rejected by the judge, and he drew a tough prosecutor and a lengthy prison sentence. Reidel and Mitakis, who were more hardened and astute, fared better in the end, while the generous and amiable Soudan was forced to bear much of the burden. Gregariousness and exaggeration may have contributed to his ascent, but they became tragic flaws which then led to charges of misrepresentation and fraud. Ironically, the *Salem* affair had its antecendents in the tumultuous civil war in Lebanon; later, a Lebanese immigrant to America received the harshest punishment as a legal transgressor. Full circle, dust to dust.

The Target

Fraud may be defined as 'the intentional deception of another person through means such as lying and cheating for the purpose of deriving an unjust personal, social, political, or economic advantage over that other person.' From a legal perspective, the emphasis is on whatever 'undue advantage' is gained, as the morality of lying or practicing deceit is another matter altogether.[1] Species of fraud which appear germane to the *Salem* case are making false and misleading statements, false pretenses (misrepresenting facts in order to get another's goods or money), false representation (upon which another relies to his detriment), falsification (such as tampering with a document), fraudulent concealment (of vital information affecting a contract) and fraudulent conversion (another's property is put to your own use).[2] Not only did fraud penetrate at so many levels vertically, but it was also evident horizontally in terms of targets and geographical scope of operations. As an article in a legal journal asserted: 'Even a fairly straightforward maritime fraud may well cross the boundaries of many traditional industries and involve the misuse of various facets of the international trade transaction. In the *Salem*, the fraudsters employed puppet companies, forged bills of lading, numbered bank accounts into which letters of credit were paid, and a ship that changed name and register – thereby involving innocent shippers, consigness, consignors, agents, insurers and traversing many national jurisdictions.' The authors referred to the perpetrators as 'cosmopolitan crooks' who took advantage of lawful practices in many industries to further their own fraudulent aims.[3]

The *Salem* fraud compromised controls, and possibly personnel too. It was facilitated by South Africa's secrecy laws and oil procurement system, which almost invited illegality in the quest for oil sufficiency. South Africa was intentionally chosen as the prime target, and those who impose the oil embargo against the apartheid state have probably come to realize that such illegality has become part of South Africa's added cost in terms of driving up oil import prices and victimizing her through fraud.

Despite its protestations, South Africa was certainly a victim of the *Salem* conspiracy to the tune of $30.5 million extra paid for the cargo. Shell, after being reimbursed by the South Africans and collecting on two insurance policies, lost about $16 million; while the cargo insurers were out approximately $10 million. The hull insurance broker, Lowndes Lambert, was set back over $300,000 so a grand total for the *Salem* fraud would be roughly $57 million. On top of this figure must be added the extensive cost of investigations carried out by Britain, the United States, the Netherlands, Greece, South Africa, Senegal, Liberia and both the cargo and hull insurers, plus the outlays for trials in several countries. The fraud could even have been $24 million greater due to a hull insurance claim had not the *British Trident* arrived in the nick of time.

While the basic fraud may have been for $57 million, the perpetrators received only $32 million, as the loss of the scuttled ship and the price differential on the cargo between what Shell paid Pontoil and what the SFF paid Beets must be taken into account. From that $32 million must be subtracted numerous expenses such as air flights, hotels, telexes and other communications, legal fees, interest charges, wages and payoffs to the crew, commissions, introduction fees, possible bribes in Liberia and Senegal, the purchase of Oxford Shipping, the establishment of Shipomex, and payment of the first hull insurance premium. In addition, Soudan rewarded the employees of American Polamax and had some of his bank accounts frozen. Reidel claims that Beets Trading even paid taxes on the *Salem* proceeds to Switzerland! While the fraud was surely lucrative, large sums had to be expended and the spoils were shared by many.

Aftermath

The *Salem* went down at a time when prospects for the shipping industry were starting to get brighter. A reduced incidence of maritime fraud could have been anticipated due to changing economic circumstances, but the *Salem* case had a major impact as well. It was instrumental in convincing commercial interests that the International Maritime Bureau should be established, and this organization then took the lead in investigating and publicizing maritime frauds. By mid-1983, the IMB was already reporting a significant drop in scuttling, charter fraud, and documentary fraud.[4] The IMB was then active in developing the Seadocs system, which provides a central registry in London for bills of lading. They no longer have to be sent from buyer to buyer, a procedure under which the paperwork usually lagged behind the transactions, facilitating fraud. Trial testing of Seadocs began in May 1985, and the system started to operate in 1987.

Insurers, hard hit by escalating claims, sought to protect themselves by changing the cargo clauses associated with the standard Lloyd's policy. 'Takings at sea' were removed as basic risks, although extra coverage for them was still available at a higher premium. The new guidelines became effective in January 1982, but policies including the former provisions were to remain valid through March 1983. Insurers benefited, but cargo owners found little solace as the applicability of Shell's line of legal argumentation in the Gibbs case became more limited.

Steps taken in the commercial sector were not matched by political cooperation to stamp out maritime fraud as states feared any encroachment upon their sovereignty. A resolution adopted by the Twelfth Assembly of the Inter-Governmental Consultative Organization (IMCO) in November 1981 stated that the organization 'recognizes the important and crucial role which self-regulation by the relevant commercial and industrial interests must play in combating maritime fraud in all its forms.'[5] Vaguely, governments were called upon to cooperate to prevent such fraud, but IMCO's stance was essentially one of passing the buck. The next two Assembly sessions in 1983 and 1985 failed to pay any attention to the issue. Similarly, the UN Conference on Trade and Development (UNCTAD) did not press for reforms. Finally, in February 1984, it organized a conference on maritime fraud in Geneva, but political squabbles broke out between developed and developing countries on the degree of action to be taken. In general, the developed countries were unwilling to have their nationals placed within the jurisdiction of courts in Third World states, so they opposed any facilitation of extradition. Ironically, most of the financial losses through fraud were incurred in the more developed states. UNCTAD shied away from future conferences on the subject and attempted to save face by having its shipping committee look into the problem.[6]

The shipping, oil and insurance trades have traditionally been conducted in a gentlemanly manner that may not be suitable in the present environment of reckless competition and trans-national crime. In the insurance and oil industries, deals are considered formalized well before the exchange of documents. Among shippers and commodities traders, documents are often supplied late and there has been some laxity regarding bills of lading. Effective controls have not yet been established (although the Seadocs system is a step in the right direction). Shipowners may hide behind foreign corporate registrations or management companies, names of vessels may easily be changed, countries like South Africa may refuse to list tanker calls, and cargo insurance policies provide little protection against the criminal actions of shipowners. In addition, casual supervision of ports almost condones the practices of false certification and 'topping'.

Investigating and prosecuting maritime fraud are rendered extremely difficult, as many oil and shipping companies (and

South Africa too) reject any intrusion into their affairs. States often have little incentive to get involved as the insurance is usually placed in London and they do not want to bother indicting foreign nationals whose crimes were committed at sea. In any case, extraditing the necessary witnesses is nearly impossible. Flag states are reluctant to offend shippers or precipitate a drop in registrations, and they usually have to contend with non-citizen officers and crews. Where a flag of convenience is concerned, most open registration states other than Liberia do not have sufficient investigatory machinery, nor do they have effective jurisdiction over shipowners and managers who reside elsewhere. In the *Salem* case, Liberia had extraterritorial control over the tanker and could have prosecuted Georgoulis and Kalomiropoulos. It could also have sought the extradition of additional crew members as it had workable treaties with many countries. However, nothing could have been done in regard to Fred Soudan, the owner of the vessel. Oxford Shipping was registered in Liberia, but there was no legal requirement to list shareholders or officers. Only an anonymous corporate entity could be punished by fining or cancellation of registration, but Soudan personally was not liable to Liberian justice, as only his corporation had legal standing, not individuals. Attempting to prosecute a particular person was useless, as he could always resign from the corporation.[7]

Systemic flaws still exist. A fraud similar to the *Salem* can therefore happen again, just as Watergate was followed by Irangate and banks may be robbed for a second time. Security is not invincible, and human nature surely bears imperfections. One must also realize that ship and cargo owners are not unduly alarmed by fraud as they are backed by insurance that frequently exceeds the value of their hulls and cargoes. Oil prices are low and a shipping lull is now expected to affect both the crude and dry bulk carriers until at least 1990. Maritime crime may thus experience a resurgence, for it has been with us throughout recorded history. Captain Anastasios Tzamtzis has written about a cargo fraud and attempted scuttling in the fourth century BC. It involved a voyage from Syracuse to Piraeus and was mentioned in a court address by the famous Greek orator, Demosthenes.[8]

Maritime fraud is as eternal as the sea. Whether a tranquil surface or raging whitecaps meet the eye, scuttled ships from generations of scheming mariners lie concealed below. The *Salem*

126

has now joined them in their subterranean burial ground and, in the spirit of Melville's *Moby Dick*, the great shroud of the sea rolls on as it has for thousands of years.

■ Notes

High Drama at Sea

1 Logbook of *British Trident*, January 17 1980, Exhibit 1036, *U.S. v. Soudan*: statement by Captain Taylor, May 7 1980, Exhibit 1041, ibid.; and statement by Barbara Padfield, radio officer of *British Trident*, Exhibit 1063, ibid.
2 Exhibit 1041, op. cit.; Liberian examination of Dimitrios Georgoulis, March 14 1980, Exhibit-1117, *U.S. v. Soudan*, op. cit.; Liberian examination of Antonios Kalomiropoulos, March 15 1980, Exhibit 1120, ibid.; and statement by P.A. Martin, chief officer of the *British Trident*, Exhibit 1064, ibid.
3 *Panorama*, BBC1 Television, August 18 1980, p. 8.
4 Report by Captain Taylor, January 18 1980, Exhibit 1043, *U.S. v. Soudan*, op. cit.
5 Exhibit 1063, op. cit.; statement by P.C. Warren, chief engineer of the *British Trident*, Exhibit 1066, *U.S. v. Soudan*, op. cit., and Exhibit 1041, op. cit.
6 Exhibit 1064, op. cit.; 'Interim report of preliminary investigation into the sinking of the Liberian tanker Salem', Republic of Liberia, Bureau of Maritime Affairs, April 1980, pp. 11 and 18; and *Panorama*, op. cit., p. 8.
7 Exhibit 1040, op. cit.
8 B. Conway, *The Piracy Business*, Middlesex, Hamlyn, 1981, p. 77, and E. Ellen and D. Campbell, *International Maritime Fraud*, London, Sweet & Maxwell, 1981, p. 58.
9 Exhibit 1117, op. cit. and *U.S. v. Soudan*, op. cit., vol. XV, pp. 94 and 100.
10 This phrase was popularized by a BBC television documentary on August 18 1980, and then used widely by the media.

The Plot Takes Shape

1 Articles of incorporation were signed on July 7 1978, but the firm was not formally incorporated until February 9 1979.

2 *Panorama*, BBC1 Television, August 18 1980, p. 2 and G. Laam and R. Robijns, 'Het geheim van de verdwenen supertanker', *Haagse Post*, December 13 1980, p. 55.
3 *U.S. v. Soudan*, vol. XXXIII, p. 65.
4 Ibid., vol. XXIX, p. 116.
5 Ibid., p. 137 and Government's trial memorandum, U.S. District Court for the Southern District of Texas, Houston Division, *U.S. v. Soudan*, p. 3.
6 *U.S. v. Soudan*, op. cit., vol. XXIX, p. 122; *Lloyd's List*, February 6 1986, p. 1; and P.C. Swanepoel, 'Report on the circumstances surrounding the sale of the cargo of crude oil on board the vessel SALEM to South Africa in 1979', November 18, 1983, pp. 5-10 and 25-26. This source will hereafter be cited as the 'Swanepoel report'. About October 3, Reidel presented an offer of oil at the South African embassy in the Hague. Also in October, he offered the oil to a Madrid broker, Laurence Smith. See ibid., pp. 28 and 32-4.
7 *U.S. v. Soudan*, op. cit., vol. IV, pp. 201-2, 209 and 213-14 and 'Swanepoel report', op. cit., pp. 13 and 21-2.
8 *U.S. v. Soudan*, op. cit., vol. III, pp. 110 and 120.
9 Ibid., vol. XXXIII, pp. 11, 15, 18, 21 and 65 and 'Swanepoel report', op. cit., pp. 16 and 20.
10 *U.S. v. Soudan*, op. cit., vol. I, pp. 6-9 and vol. II, pp. 31 and 42.
11 Ibid., vol. XVII, p. 76.
12 Report by Peter Griggs, Metropolitan and City Police Company Fraud Department, New Scotland Yard, June 10 1980 (as presented at the trial of Fred Soudan), p. 15.
13 *U.S. v. Soudan*, op. cit., vol. I, p. 11. At first, Soudan indicated that Von Lange's company, Intma, was to be the charterer of the tanker. See 'Swanepoel report', op. cit., pp. 139-40.
14 Interview with John Masters, January 22, 1987 and 'Swanepoel report', op. cit., pp. 139-40.
15 Griggs' report, op. cit., p. 49 and Laam and Robijns, op. cit., p. 56. The passport indicates that it was issued to 'Bert Samuel Stein' in Frankfurt on May 25 1976. Later, at his trial in Greece, Mitakis was accused of providing this passport.
16 *U.S. v. Soudan*, op. cit., vol. XXX, p. 7.
17 Georgoulis had no experience as master of a supertanker and it is possible that he and Annivas went to Singapore for a brief training course.
18 *U.S. v. Soudan*, op. cit. vol. XXXIII, pp. 42-3 and 72-3; 'Interim report of preliminary investigation into the sinking of the Liberian tanker Salem', Republic of Liberia, Bureau of Maritime Affairs, April 1980, p. 6; and E. Ellen and D. Campbell, *International Maritime Fraud*, London, Sweet & Maxwell, 1981, p. 55.
19 *Sunday Express*, August 26 1984 and 'Swanepoel report', op. cit., pp. 119, 173, 271 and 276. Before contacting Shorrock, Soudan had made an unsuccessful attempt to sell oil to South Africa. See ibid., p. 30.
20 'Swanepoel report', op. cit., pp. 37-9 and 43 and trial memorandum, op. cit., p. 6.

NOTES

21 Ibid., p. 8 and minutes of October 15 meeting, Exhibit 864B, *U.S. v. Soudan*, op. cit.
22 'Swanepoel report', op. cit., pp. 43-50.
23 Memorandum of agreement between American Polamax and SFF, October 16 1979, Exhibit 865, *U.S. v. Soudan*, op. cit.; trial memorandum, op. cit., pp. 8-9; 'Swanepoel report', op. cit., p. 53; and *U.S. v. Soudan*, op. cit., vol. XXII, p. 204.
24 Ibid., vol. XXXIII, pp. 22-6 and 42-3; trial memorandum, op. cit., pp. 10-11; and 'Swanepoel report', op. cit., p. 15.
25 Ibid., p. 91.
26 Trial memorandum, op. cit., pp. 12-13; *U.S. v. Soudan*, op. cit., vol. I pp. 17-18, vol. IV, pp. 67-8 and vol. III, pp. 150 and 153; and *Financial Mail*, March 18 1983, p. 1181.
27 *U.S. v. Soudan*, op. cit., vol. I, p. 18 and vol. IV, pp. 67-85.
28 Speech by Dr Dirk Mostert, Johannesburg, August 23 1984, p. 23. A South African newspaper claimed that the South African navy was prepared to intercept the tanker if it failed to deliver the oil. See *The Citizen*, August 27 1984.
29 SFF memorandum, March 9 1983, pp. 14-15.
30 'Swanepoel report', op. cit., p. 176.
31 *U.S. v. Soudan*, op. cit., vol. III, pp. 160-61 and *Financial Mail*, op. cit.

Laying the Groundwork

1 The deadweight tonnage represents the storage capacity of the vessel by weight, including cargo, bunkers and provisions. The gross tonnage refers to the storage capacity in cubic feet divided by one hundred.
2 'Swanepoel report', p. 146. Earlier, the *Sirius* had been considered by Soudan and Masters. Note that the *South Sun* should not be confused with the *Southern Sun*, a tanker that was severely damaged in November 1976 when it ran aground off Zueitina, Libya.
3 N. Ash, 'The sinking of the Salem: accident or design?', *8 Days*, vol. 2, no. 13, March 29 1980, pp. 6-11 and 58-9; interview with John Masters, January 22, 1987; and 'Swanepoel report', op. cit., pp. 146, 275 and 286. Some of the details of the sales agreement had been worked out by November 20, prior to Mercabank's offer of a letter of credit. See Exhibit 1001, *U.S. v. Soudan*.
4 Testimony of John Masters, ibid., vol. VII, pp. 18-20.
5 Ibid., pp. 24 and 41 and 'Swanepoel report', op. cit., p. 149.
6 *U.S. v. Soudan*, op. cit., vol. IX, pp. 97 and 103.
7 Ibid., vol. I, p. 19; agreement to purchase Oxford Shipping, November 27 1979, Exhibit 55, ibid.; and E. Ellen and D. Campbell, *International Maritime Fraud*, London, Sweet & Maxwell, 1981, p. 56.
8 G. Laam and R. Robijns, 'Het geheim van de verdwenen super-

tanker', *Haagse Post*, December 13 1980, pp. 56-7 and Report by Peter Griggs, 'Metropolitan and City Police Company Fraud Department, New Scotland Yard, June 10 1980 (as presented at the trial of Fred Soudan), pp. 49-50. The certificate of incorporation for Shipomex lists Osterkamp as president and 'Stein' as secretary. See 'Swanepoel report', op. cit., p. 147. The allegation that Frey was convicted of fraud is in Griggs' report, op. cit., p. 49.

9 Oxford-Shipomex agreement, dated November 26 1979, Exhibit 61, *U.S. v. Soudan*, op. cit.; ibid., vol. XXXI, p. 195; *Het Vrije Volk*, April 7 1983; and 'Swanepoel report', op. cit., pp. 136-7, 178 and 282.

10 Reidel-Soudan agreement and annex, November 25 1979, Exhibits 50A and 50B, *U.S. v. Soudan*, op. cit. The agreement is witnessed by Mitakis and Attar, and the annex by Mitakis. Reidel claims that Mitakis actually drew up the agreements and signed them, but was not present when Soudan met with Reidel. See *U.S. v. Soudan*, ibid., vol. XXX, pp. 16-17.

11 Testimony of John Masters, ibid., vol. VII, pp. 18-20.

12 On November 7, Reidel telexed Soudan to say that the *South Sun* could arrive at Dar es Salaam on November 9. On November 13, he telexed Naude and gave the date as November 14. See 'Swanepoel report', op. cit., pp. 73 and 79.

13 Liberian examination of Georgoulis, March 14 1980, Exhibit 1117, *U.S. v. Soudan* op. cit. One author maintained that Georgoulis had a bona fide Liberian master's certificate, but it was not really his. A British newspaper suggested that he had a fake Liberian master's certificate bearing a number belonging to a Pakistani engineer. See B. Conway, *The Piracy Business*, Middlesex, Hamlyn, 1981, p. 70 and *Sunday Times*, February 3 1980, p. 3.

14 Liberia's marine safety investigator in Greece, Anastasios Tzamtzis, charged that Georgoulis was connected to thefts aboard the *Betty, Marianne*, and *Alexandros K*. See *Daily Telegraph*, February 6 1980 and C. Dobson and R. Payne, 'Pirates who prey on the world's ships', *Now*, February 15 1980, p. 23.

15 Ellen and Campbell, op. cit., p. 56; Conway, op. cit., p. 70; *Lloyd's List*, February 8 1980, p. 8; *The Observer*, February 24 1980; Dobson and Payne, op.cit. p. 23; letter from Anastasios Tzamtzis, February 27 1987; and letter from Gillian Whitakker, March 6 1987. Georgoulis does not appear to have been the master of the *Alexandros K*. when it sank.

16 *The Observer*, op. cit.; Ellen and Campbell, op. cit., p. 56; Conway, op. cit., p. 71; and Tzamtzis letter, op. cit.

17 *U.S. v. Soudan*, op. cit., vol. XIV, pp. 11-17 and 'Swanepoel report', op. cit., pp. 200, 211 and 214.

18 Ibid., pp. 199 and 218 and *U.S. v. Soudan*, op. cit., vol. XIV, pp. 26 and 83.

19 Ibid., p. 30 and charter party agreement of November 29 1979, Exhibit 941, *U.S. v. Soudan*, op. cit.

20 I. Middleton and A. Renouf, 'Salem – the aftermath', *Seatrade*, February 1980, p. 13 and interview with Peter Griggs, December 15 1986.

NOTES

21 Exhibits 913 a and b and 945, *U.S. v. Soudan*, op. cit.
22 'Swanepoel report', op. cit., pp. 54-6, 59-60, 68, 71-2, 74, 272 and 275.
23 Ibid., pp. 79 and 274.
24 Ibid., pp. 75-7 and 122.
25 Ibid., p. 272.
26 Ibid., p. 93; *U.S. v. Soudan*, op. cit., vol. I, p. 23; and Government's trial memorandum, US District Court for the Southern District of Texas, Houston Division, *U.S. v. Soudan*, p. 15.
27 Ash, op. cit., p. 8; 'Interim report of preliminary investigation into the sinking of the Liberian tanker Salem', Republic of Liberia, Bureau of Maritime Affairs, April 1980, p. 8; and *U.S. v. Soudan*, op. cit., vol. I, p. 24.

The Payoff

1 Exhibits 897 and 899, *U.S. v. Soudan*.
2 'Interim report of preliminary investigation into the sinking of the Liberian tanker Salem', Republic of Liberia, Bureau of Maritime Affairs, April 1980, p. 8; *U.S. v. Soudan*, op. cit., vol. I, p. 24; and 'Swanepoel report', p. 138. Evidence about the electrician's wife, Maria Papaleon, appears in Report by Peter Griggs, Metropolitan and City Police Company Fraud Department, New Scotland Yard, June 10 1980 (as presented at the trial of Fred Soudan), p. 38. A Tunisian seaman on the *Salem* reported that the cook's wife departed in Kuwait, but he did not assert that the electrician's wife left the ship. See statement by Tunisian seaman, January 1980, p. 2.
3 Testimony of John Dale, *U.S. v. Soudan*, op. cit., vol. XVII, pp. 166-7 and 170; and M. Brody, 'Boom in piracy', *Barron's*, November 29 1982, p. 18.
4 E. Ellen and D. Campbell, *International Maritime Fraud*, London, Sweet & Maxwell, 1981, p. 7; *Daily Telegraph*, February 9 1980; and 'Swanepoel report', op. cit., p. 206.
5 Speech by Dr Dirk Mostert, Johannesburg, August 23 1984, p. 34.
6 'Swanepoel report', op. cit., p. 197.
7 Ibid., pp. 198 and 224-31.
8 J. Knox, 'Shell International Petroleum Co. v. Gibbs: Lloyd's S.G. policy walks the plank', *Texas International Law Journal*, vol. 19, no. 1, winter 1984, p. 165.
9 'Swanepoel report', op. cit., pp. 94-8.
10 *Lloyd's List*, February 6 1986, p. 1 and February 7, pp. 1 and 10; *Deegblad Scheepvaart*, February 6 and 7 1986; interview with Peter Griggs, December 15 1986; *U.S. v. Soudan*, op. cit., vol. I p. 25; and 'Swanepoel report', op. cit., pp. 102 and 107.
11 Exhibition 51, *U.S. v. Soudan*, op. cit., *Deegblad Scheepvaart*, February 7 1986, op. cit., and 'Swanepoel report', op. cit., p. 276.

12 Exhibit 51, op. cit. and 'Swanepoel report', op. cit., p. 104.
13 See 'Shell International Petroleum Company Ltd. v. Gibbs', *The All England Law Reports Annotated*, vol. 1, 1982, p. 244.
14 'Swanepoel report', op. cit., p. 81.
15 'Interim report', op. cit., p. 19.
16 *U.S. v. Soudan*, op. cit., vol. XXII, p. 31 and vol. XXXI, p. 9; and Mostert speech, op. cit., p. 2.
17 'Swanepoel report', op. cit., pp. 113, 117 and 124-5.
18 *U.S. v. Soudan*, op. cit., vol. I, p. 30; Griggs' interview, op. cit.; Griggs' report, op. cit., p. 41; B. Conway, *The Piracy Business*, Middlesex, Hamlyn 1981, p. 74; 'Swanepoel report', op. cit., p. 130; and statement by Tunisian seaman, op. cit., p. 5.
19 Kalomiropoulos testimony of May 22 1986 in letter from Gillian Whitakker, March 6, 1987 and statement by Tunisian seaman, op. cit., p. 6.
20 *Lloyd's Register of Ships, 1979-80*; Conway, op. cit., p. 86; 'Crude oil deliveries to South Africa from Brunei', Amsterdam, Shipping Research Bureau, January 1987, p. 19; and 'Swanepoel report', op. cit., p. 270.
21 Ibid., p. 93 and Government's trial memorandum, US District Court for the Southern District of Texas, Houston Division, *U.S. v. Soudan*, p. 14 and 'Swanepoel report', op. cit., p. 93.
22 SFF memorandum, March 9, 1983, p. 10 and 'Shell International Petroleum Company Ltd. v. Gibbs', op. cit., p. 231.
23 'Distribution of funds from Salem transaction to Fred Soudan and others', Exhibit 15, *U.S. v. Soudan*, op. cit.
24 Ibid., *NRC Handelsblad*, February 6 1986; *De Telegraaf*, January 26 1985; Griggs' report, op. cit., p. 55; *Lloyd's List*, February 7 1986, p. 10; *Sunday Times*, February 3 1980, p. 3; *Het Vrije Volk*, February 6 1986; and 'Swanepoel report', op. cit., pp. 284-5.
25 Griggs's report, op. cit., p. 53.
26 G. Laam and R. Robijns, 'Het geheim van de verdwenen supertanker', *Haagse Post*, December 13 1980, p. 63; *Panorama*, BBC1 Television, August 18 1980, p. 9; and *Lloyd's List*, February 14 1986, p. 1. According to the report on his *Salem* investigation by J.C. Montgomery, Liberia's Deputy Commissioner of Maritime Affairs, Georgoulis was given $220,000 before leaving Greece, while chief mate Annivas received $750,000 once the oil was delivered. See 'Report on Salem investigation trip, March 22-31, 1980', p. 3.
27 *U.S. v. Soudan*, op. cit., vol. I, p. 27 and vol. XVI, p. 113; *Newsletter on the Oil Embargo Against South Africa*, no. 5, September 1986, p. 10; and *Lloyd's List*, May 24 1986, p. 1.
28 Ibid.; Panorama, op. cit., p. 10; and letter from Anastasios Tzamtzis, April 8 1987.
29 *Lloyd's List*, March 8 1985 and *Het Vrije Volk*, op. cit. This money may have been used to make payments in South Africa.
30 Panorama, op. cit., pp. 1-3, 8 and 11.
31 *Het Vrije Volk*, op. cit. and *NRC Handelsblad*, op. cit.
32 See Exhibit 15, op. cit.
33 *Lloyd's List* February 16 1985, p. 3.

Dénouement

1 *U.S. v Soudan*, vol. I, p. 30 and B. Conway, *The Piracy Business*, Middlesex, Hamlyn, 1981, p. 75.
2 Statement by Tunisian seaman, January 1980, pp. 4-5.
3 Ibid., pp. 6-10.
4 Interview with Peter Griggs, December 15 1986; statement of Captain Robert Taylor, May 7 1980, Exhibit 1041 and telex from Lowndes Lambert to Soudan, Exhibit 803, *U.S. v. Soudan*, op. cit.; *Lloyd's List*, January 19 1980, p. 6; and *Lloyd's Register of Shipping Casualty Return* (through March 31 1980), p. 10.
5 Exhibit 1041, op. cit.
6 'Interim report of preliminary investigation into the sinking of the Liberian tanker Salem', Republic of Liberia, Bureau of Maritime Affairs, April 1980, p. 13; *Sunday Times*, February 3 1980, p. 3; Report by Peter Griggs, Metropolitan and City Police Company Fraud Department, New Scotland Yard, June 10 1980 (as presented at the trial of Fred Soudan), p. 47; and statement by Tunisian seamen, op. cit., p. 10.
7 'Swanepoel report', p. 97.
8 *U.S. v. Soudan*, op. cit. vol. IX, pp. 118-19.
9 Letter from Triandafilou to Liberian Services, December 24 1979, Exhibit 1057, *U.S. v. Soudan*, op. cit.
10 *U.S. v. Soudan*, op. cit., vol. XXX, pp. 139-40 and vol. IX, pp. 124 and 133; Reidel telex to Avgerinos and Triandafilou, December 26 1979, Exhibit 988, ibid.; and Griggs's report, op. cit., p. 62.
11 *U.S. v. Soudan*, op. cit., vol. XIX, p. 124.
12 Ibid., vol. IX, p. 125; Conway, op. cit., p. 74; and Soudan writ filed January 4 1980 in Supreme Court of the State of New York.
13 Soudan's terms for selling the ship to Reidel, December 28 1979, Exhibit 798, *U.S. v. Soudan*, op. cit., Reidel later claimed that he planned to give the ship to Mitakis. See ibid., vol. XXX, p. 36.
14 Soudan writ, op. cit. and Griggs's report, op. cit., p. 56.
15 'Interim report,' op. cit., pp. 21-2, and 'Swanepoel report', op. cit., pp. 188-9.
16 *U.S. v. Soudan*, op. cit., vol. IX, pp. 142-3, and vol. XXX, p. 144; and statement by Northern Ships, January 11 1980, Exhibit 57, ibid.
17 Soudan statements of January 15 1980, Exhibit 996 and Soudan telex to John Masters, Exhibit 794, ibid.; and 'Swanepoel report', op. cit., p. 118. The telex to the SFF was preceded by a phone call on the same matter the previous day. See ibid., p. iv.
18 Soudan agreement with Reidel, January 12 1980, Exhibit 797 and Reidel telex to Soudan, January 16 1980, Exhibit 796, *U.S. v. Soudan*, op. cit.
19 Soudan telex to Reidel, January 17 1980, Exhibit 801; Reidel telex to Soudan, January 18 1980, Exhibit 804; and Soudan telex to Reidel, January 18 1980, Exhibit 805, ibid.
20 See ibid., vol. XX, pp. 127-8.

21 Soudan telex to Reidel, December 12 1979, Exhibit 789, ibid.; Griggs's report, op. cit., p. 62; and 'Swanepoel report', op. cit., p. 266.
22 *U.S. v. Soudan*, op. cit., vol. XXIII, pp. 66-7. A spokesman for Shell claimed that his company was not aware until January 25 of the visit to South Africa. See ibid., vol. XVII, p. 176.
23 See 'Swanepoel report', op. cit., p. 210.
24 Interview with Lee Coppack, former insurance correspondent of *Lloyd's List*, November 19, 1986 and E. Ellen and D. Campbell, *International Maritime Fraud*, London, Sweet & Maxwell, 1981, p. 7.
25 G. Laam and R. Robijns, 'Het geheim van de verdwenen super-tanker', *Haagse Post*, December 13 1980, p. 56.
26 Admiralty Court, Queen's Bench Division, 1980, Folio 69 and Commercial Court, Queen's Bench Division, Action no. 1980 S, no. 4211.
27 *Wall Street Journal*, February 7 and 8 1980.
28 *U.S. v. Soudan*, op. cit., vol. XXIII, pp. 70-1.
29 Interviews with Coppack, op. cit. and Kenneth Mayer, Lowndes Lambert Marine Ltd, November 13 1986.
30 Ibid., Coppack, op. cit.; B. Abrahamsson, *International Ocean Shipping: Current Concepts and Principles*, Boulder, Westview, 1980, p. 103; and G. Hodgson, *Lloyd's of London*, London, Penguin, 1986, p. 102.
31 Mayer, op. cit. and Coppack, op. cit.
32 *U.S. v. Soudan*, op. cit., vol. I p. 33.
33 Exhibit 801, op. cit. and ibid., vol. XX, p. 124.
34 Coppack, op. cit. and *Lloyd's List*, August 6 1980, p. 1.
35 Speech by Dr Dirk Mostert, Johannesburg, August 23 1984, p. 31.
36 *U.S. v. Soudan*, op. cit., vol. XVII, pp. 36-8.
37 Mayer, op. cit.; Coppack, op. cit.; and R.J. Lambeth, *Templeman on Marine Insurance*, London, Pitman, 1986, pp. 17 and 448.
38 Mayer, op. cit. and Coppack op. cit. Soudan also arranged for Protection and Indemnity coverage, and again did not report his bareboat charter agreement. See Griggs's report, op. cit., p. 26.
39 *Lloyd's List*, February 13 1986, p. 3.
40 Ibid., February 14 1986, p. 1.
41 *U.S. v. Soudan*, op. cit., vol. XIX, p. 173 and vol. VII, pp. 30-4.
42 Ibid., vol. VIII, p. 25.
43 Exhibit 796, op. cit. and ibid., vol. XX, pp. 127-8.
44 Ibid., vol. X, p. 14 and vol. XXII, p. 55; Griggs's report, op. cit., p. 28; and 'Swanepoel report', op. cit., p. iv.
45 *U.S. v. Soudan*, op. cit, vol. VII, pp. 18-20.
46 Ibid., vol. XXII, p. 172.
47 *Newsletter on the Oil Embargo Against South Africa*, vol. I, no. 2, June 1985, p. 4.
48 *U.S. v. Soudan*, op. cit., vol. XX, pp. 127-30.
49 *Lloyd's List*, August 6 1980, p. 1.
50 Ibid., February 7 1980, p. 1.
51 *U.S. v. Soudan*, op. cit., vol. XVII, p. 103.
52 Statement by Tunisian seaman, op. cit., p. 3.
53 'Swanepoel report', op. cit., 250-1.

NOTES

The Twilight World

1 A careful study published in 1972 predicted that the demand for seaborne crude oil would continue to increase up to 1980. See 'Seaborne supplies of crude oil during the 1970's: an analysis of the consequences of the energy crisis', Westinform Shipping Report no. 297, London, November 1972.
2 *The Square Mile in 1986*, London, De Montfort, 1987, p. 148.
3 *Lloyd's Register of Shipping*, Annual Report, 1975, p. 15.
4 *World Tanker Fleet Review*, August 1977, p. 26 and August, 1978, p. 31; and *Lloyd's Register of Shipping*, Annual Report, 1978, p. 6.
5 *World Tanker Fleet Review*, August 1977, p. 16; February 1978, p. 17; and August 1978, p. 15.
6 Ibid., August 1977, p. 18 and August 1978, p. 22.
7 *Lloyd's Register of Shipping*, Annual Report, 1979, p. 6 and *World Tanker Fleet Review*, August 1978, pp. 15 and 31; February 1979, pp. 15 and 22; and August 1979, pp. 16, 18 and 32.
8 'Tanker review', *Lloyd's Shipping Economist*, vol. 2, no. 1, January 1980, pp. 8-13.
9 *Lloyd's Register of Shipping*, Statistical Tables, 1978, pp. 3 and 76; 1979, pp. 3 and 76; and 1980, pp. 3 and 78; *Nautical Review*, vol. 4, no. 3, March 1980, p. 28; *IMO News*, no. 3 1984, p. 3 and no. 2, 1986, p. 16; and *Lloyd's Register of Shipping*, 1977, 1978 and 1979, tables 2A, 2B and 3.
10 B. Abrahamsson, *International Ocean Shipping: Current Concepts and Principles*, Boulder, Westview, 1980, p. 104.
11 D. Rother, *Ship Casualties – An Analysis of Causes and Circumstances*, Bremen, Institute of Shipping Economics, 1980, p. 31 and B.N. Metaxas, *Flags of Convenience*, Hants, Gower, 1985, pp. 23-5.
12 See *Lloyd's List*, October 18 1979, p. 5 and B. Conway, *the Piracy Business*, Middlesex, Hamlyn, 1981.
13 G. Hodgson, *Lloyd's of London*, London, Penguin, 1986, p. 154.
14 *IMCO News*, no. 3, 1980, p. 11 and no. 1, 1981, p. 3; *IMO News*, no. 1, 1983, p. 3; *IMCO Resolutions and Other Decisions*, Eleventh Session, London, IMCO, 1980, p. 319; and *Lloyd's List*, November 17, 1979, p. 1.
15 Ibid., January 17, 1980, p. 1.
16 'The sea gets sick but never dies', *100A1*, April 1978, pp. 2, 5 and 11.
17 Rother op. cit., p. 31 and 'Greek trading patterns', *Lloyd's Shipping Economist*, vol. 2, no. 9, September 1980, p. 13.
18 E. Ellen and D. Campbell, *International Maritime Fraud*, London, Sweet & Maxwell, 1981, p. 2 and Hodgson, op. cit., p. 177.
19 *Lloyd's List*, September 20, 1980, p. 1.
20 *Lloyd's Register of Shipping*, Statistical Tables, 1980, p. 3 and 1981, p. 3; *IMCO News*, no. 3, 1981, p. 10; *IMO News*, no. 3, 1984, p. 3 and no. 2, 1986, p. 16; and 'Greek trading patterns', op. cit., p. 13.

21 See Ellen and Campbell, op. cit., pp. 29-30.
22 For rumours about the *Irenes Serenade*'s cargo being delivered to South Africa, see *Rand Daily Mail*, June 6 1984 and *The Observer*, August 26 1984.
23 *Financial Mail*, November 9 1979, p. 623 and Advocate-General's Report, South Africa, June 27 1984, p. 9.
24 See M. Bailey, 'The impact on South Africa of the cut-off of Iranian oil', New York, Centre Against Apartheid, July 1979, p. 1; M. Bailey and B. Rivers, 'Oil sanctions against South Africa', New York: Centre Against Apartheid, June 1978, p. 5; and 'Oil sanctions against South Africa', New York, Sanctions Working Group, August 1980, p. 3.
25 *Sunday Times*, December 31 1978; *Financial Mail*, May 11 1984, p. 31; and *Africa Research Bulletin*, Economic, Financial and Technical Series, no. 9. October 31 1979, p. 5277.
26 *Windhoek Advertiser*, April 25 1986.
27 *Lloyd's List*, February 24 1979, p. 2.
28 Advocate-General's Report, op. cit., p. 8.
29 'John Deuss: Transworld Oil', Amsterdam, Shipping Research Bureau, January 1985, p. 1; Advocate-General's report, op. cit., p. 34; *The Observer*, May 19 1985; and *Newsletter on the Oil Embargo Against South Africa*, vol. I, no. 2, June 1985, p. 4.
30 *Financial Mail*, July 27 1979, p. 297.
31 *The Citizen*, January 7 1984 and *The Economist*, no. 7323, January 7 1984, p. 35.
32 *Rand Daily Mail*, May 22, 1982.
33 *Hansard*, March 9 1983, p. 2659.
34 See 'Maritime fraud', *Lloyd's Shipping Economist*, vol. 8, no. 2, February 1986, p. 8.
35 SFF memorandum, March 9 1983, p. 8.
36 For a discussion of fraud controls, see J. Bologna, *Corporate Fraud*, Boston, Butterworth, 1984, pp. 94-5.
37 Advocate-General's Report, op. cit., p. 43.
38 *Het Vrije Volk*, February 6 1986.
39 Ellen and Campbell, op. cit., p. 24.
40 *Sunday Times*, August 26 1984. Swanepoel did not accept Reidel's 'topping' claim. See 'Swanepoel report', p. 2.

Following the Trail

1 Interview with Robert Bishop, February 25 1987.
2 Statement by Tunisian seaman, January 1980, passim.
3 Ibid. See also *Lloyd's List*, January 31 1980, p. 1.
4 Interview with Barbara Conway, January 28 1987.
5 N. Ash, 'The sinking of the Salem: accident or design?', *8 Days*, vol. 2, no. 13, March 29, 1980, pp. 6-11 and 58-9, and *Panorama*, BBC1 Television, August 18 1980.

6 See M. Seward, 'Salem scam', *Oceans*, November 1985, p. 19.

7 M. Quinlan, 'Oil embargo would be impractical', *Petroleum Economist*, vol. LIII, no. 11, November 1986, pp. 401-3; Report by Peter Griggs, Metropolitan and City Police Company Fraud Department, New Scotland Yard, June 10 1980 (as presented at the trial of Fred Soudan), p. 38; 'Interim report of preliminary investigation into the sinking of the Liberian tanker Salem', Republic of Liberia, Bureau of Maritime Affairs, April 1980, p. 16; E. Ellen and D. Campbell, *International Maritime Fraud*, London, Sweet & Maxwell, 1981, p. 59; Exhibit 1023, *U.S. v. Soudan*; and interview with Peter Griggs, March 2 1987.

8 Ibid.

9 A. Renouf, 'Warrants issued in Salem case as consequences sink in', *Seatrade*, vol. 10, no. 8, August 1980, p. 65.

10 *The Shipbroker*, August 1980, p. 3.

11 G. Laam and R. Robijns, 'Het geheim van de verdwenen supertanker', *Haagse Post*, December 13 1980, p. 63; *Panorama*, op. cit., pp. 10-11; and B. Conway, *The Piracy Business*, Middlesex, Hamlyn, 1981, p. 69.

12 Laam and Robijns, op. cit., p. 63.

13 *Daily Telegraph*, February 9 1980.

14 *Sunday Express*, August 26 1984.

15 'Swanepoel report', p. 21.

16 See *U.S. v. Soudan*, op. cit., vol. XXX, p. 177.

17 *Lloyd's List*, January 29 1980, p. 8; *Daily Telegraph*, February 8 1980; and interview with Gerald Cooper, March 24 1987.

18 Ibid.

19 Ibid.; *Lloyd's List*, February 15 1980, p. 14 and February 16, p. 1; and AFP, March 11, 1980.

20 'Interim report', op. cit., p. 2.

21 Seward, op. cit., p. 20 and press release in London, February 8, 1980.

22 'Interim report', op. cit., pp. 23-4.

23 *Lloyd's List*, May 9 1980, p. 1.

24 Ibid., June 12 1980, p. 1 and July 22; p. 3; and *West Africa*, no. 3283, June 23 1980, p. 1156.

25 Cooper interview, op. cit. and Alfantakis letter to Doe, May 1 1980.

26 *Keesings*, XXI, April 21-7, 1975, p. 27090.

27 Alfantakis letter to Chea Cheapoo, April 25 1980, and *Kathimerini*, June 8 1980.

28 Alfantakis letters to Cheapoo, April 25 and May 5 1980; Alfantakis letter to Doe, op. cit.; Georgoulis letters to Alfantakis, April 23 and May 3, 1980; Kalomiropoulos letter to Alfantakis, April 23 1980; statement by Georgoulis's wife and Kalomiropoulos's brother, May 13 1980; and Proceedings of the Liberian Commission of Inquiry, pp. 14-19.

29 Cooper interview, op. cit. and Proceedings, op. cit., pp. 38-9.

30 Ibid., p. 56 and Report of the Salem Commission of Inquiry, May 22 1980, pp. 10-19.

31 'Shell International Petroleum Company Ltd. v. Gibbs', *The All*

England Law Reports Annotated, vol. 1, 1982, p. 1060; Conway, op. cit., p. 82; *Panorama*, op. cit., p. 9.

32 *Lloyd's List* July 18 1980, p. 2 and M. Bailey, 'Truth about Salem oil leaks out', *New Statesman*, vol. 105, no. 2718, April 22 1983, p. 4.

33 See Seward, op. cit., p. 20.

34 *Lloyd's List*, June 26 1980, p. 1, June 27, p. 1 and September 13, p. 1; Cooper interview, op. cit.; and Cooper telex, June 25 1980.

35 *Lloyd's List*, February 6 1980, p. 1.

36 *U.S. v. Soudan*, op. cit., vol. XXII, p. 172, and speech by Dr Dirk Mostert, Johannesburg, August 23 1984, p. 12.

37 SFF memorandum, March 9 1983, p. 14 and Mostert speech, op. cit., p. 13.

38 *U.S. v. Soudan*, op. cit., vol. XVI, p. 12 and *Financial Mail*, April 11 1980, p. 123.

39 *Lloyd's List*, August 24 1984, p. 1.

40 Mostert speech, op. cit., p. 12.

41 Ibid., p. 11.

42 See John Malcomess, *Hansard*, May 4 1984, p. 84 and Mostert speech, op. cit., p. 13.

43 SFF memorandum, op. cit., p. 4 and Mostert speech, op. cit., p. 34.

44 *Lloyd's List*, February 2 1980, p. 1; Mostert speech, op. cit., p. 29; *U.S. v. Soudan*, op. cit., vol. XI, p. 54; 'Swanepoel report', op. cit., pp. 110-11; and C. Hill, 'Lading bill security – is there any?', *Seatrade*, vol. 10, no. 9, September 1980, p. 75.

45 SFF memorandum, op. cit., p. 15.

46 Advocate-General's Report, June 27 1984, p. 5; *Hansard*, March 9 1983, p. 2668 and April 26 1984, p. 5215.

47 Interview with Theo Nijenhuis, January 7 1987; interview with Robert Bishop, February 25 1987; interview with Peter Griggs, March 2 1987; *U.S. v. Soudan*, op. cit., vol. XI, p. 25; and 'Swanepoel report', p. 305.

48 Ibid.

49 *Argus*, April 12 1984.

50 *Sunday Times*, July 11 1982, p. 4.

51 SFF memorandum, op. cit., p. 17.

52 *Hansard*, March 9 1983, passim. The quotation appears on p. 2608.

53 Ibid., pp. 2630-31.

54 Ibid., April 25 1984, p. 5077.

55 Ibid., p. 5077 and April 27, p. 5294; *Rand Daily Mail*, July 13 1984; and *Financial Mail*, May 11 1984, p. 30.

56 *Hansard*, April 27 1984, p. 5295.

57 Ibid., p. 5297 and April 26, p. 5218.

58 Advocate-General's Report, op. cit., p. 43.

59 *The Star*, August 25 1984.

60 Mostert speech, op. cit., pp. 2, 8 and 17.

61 *Hansard*, May 20 1985, pp. 5855-7.

NOTES

Barristers at Work

1 'Shell International Petroleum Company Ltd. v. Gibbs', *The All England Law Reports Annotated*, vol. 1, 1982, p. 228.
2 *Lloyd's List*, April 10 1981, p. 1.
3 Ibid., February 26 1981, p. 1 and February 27, p. 1.
4 'Shell v. Gibbs', op. cit., pp. 241-2 and editorial, 'Maritime fraud', *The Journal of Business Law*, July 1982, p. 267.
5 'Shell v. Gibbs', op. cit., pp. 1062-3 and 1068-74.
6 Ibid., pp. 1062-3 and 1068; J. Knox, 'Shell International Petroleum Co. v. Gibbs: Lloyd's S.G. policy walks the plank', *Texas International Law Journal*, vol. 19, no. 1, winter 1984, pp. 173-7; and *Financial Times*, February 16 1982. The *Shell v. Gibbs* judgement was cited in June 1982 in the Commercial Court, Queen's Bench Division case of *Athens Maritime Enterprises Corporation v. Hellenic Mutual War Risks Association (Bermuda) Ltd.*
7 A. Renouf, 'Lords sinks Shell's final Salem plea', *Seatrade*, vol. 13, no. 3, March 1983, p. 91.
8 Knox, op. cit., p. 181.
9 'Shell International Petroleum Company Ltd. v. Gibbs', *All England Law Reports Annotated*, vol. 1, 1983, pp. 745-53, *The Times*, February 18 1983, p. 19; *Lloyd's List*, January 18 1983, p. 2; J. Hunt, 'Case notes: marine insurance', *Journal of Maritime Law and Commerce*, vol. 14, no. 4, October 1983, p. 608; and R.J. Lambeth, *Templeman on Marine Insurance*, London, Pitman, 1986, p. 203.
10 D.G. Powles and S.J. Hazelwood, 'Maritime fraud', *The Journal of Business Law*, May 1984, p. 244.

Days in Court

1 *Lloyd's List* February 15 1985, p. 3.
2 *Trouw*, May 4 1984; *Algemeen Dagblad*, May 3 1984 and *De Volkskrant*, December 21 1983 and February 14 1984.
3 *Trouw*, May 6 1983 and December 12 1985; *Algemeen Dagblad*, October 15 1984; and *De Volkskrant*, December 11 1985.
4 Interview with Theo Nijenhuis, January 7 1987.
5 *NRC Handelsblad*, February 6 1986.
6 *Lloyd's List*, February 6 1986, p. 14 and *Deegblad Scheepvaart*, February 6 1986.
7 *De Telegraaf*, January 26 1985.
8 *De Volkskrant*, February 6 1986 and 'Swanepoel report', p. 274.
9 *Deegblad Scheepvaart*, February 7 and 20 1986; *NRC Handelsblad*, op. cit.; *Lloyd's List*, February 6 1986, p. 1 and February 7, pp. 1 and 10; and *Het Parool*, February 6 1986.

10 *Lloyd's List*, February 20 1986, p. 1; *Deegblad Scheepvaart*, February 20 1986; *Het Parool*, op. cit.; and 'Swanepoel report', op. cit., p. 1.

11 *De Volkskrant*, May 31 1986.

12 Ibid., February 20 and 22, 1986 and letter from Theo Nijenhuis, January 10 1987. On the oil procurement activities of Bredenkamp, see *South Africa's Lifeline*, Amsterdam, Shipping Research Bureau, September 1986, p. 14.

13 *Deegblad Scheepvaart*, August 21 1986; letters from Theo Nijenhuis, January 10 and April 7 1987; Nijenhuis interview, op. cit.; and *Newsletter on the Oil Embargo Against South Africa*, no. 7, April 1987, p. 13.

14 *Deegblad Scheepvaart*, February 6 1986.

15 *Lloyd's List*, June 30 1981, p. 1. The author would like to thank *Lloyd's List* correspondent Gillian Whitakker for her generous and extensive assistance in the gathering of information on the Greek trials.

16 Ibid., June 19 1981, p. 1. In 1983, International Maritime Bureau director Eric Ellen went to Greece to encourage the opening of a trial.

17 Ibid., May 21 1983, p. 1, October 24 1983, p. 3 and November 1 1984, p. 3.

18 Ibid., April 4 1984, p. 1; letter to Greek authorities from Jenkins Scott, December 21 1984; May 21 1980 transcript of May 2 court session, People's Magisterial Court, Monrovia; and memorandum from Dunbar Innis, Monrovia City Court, October 21 1983.

19 Interview with Robert Bishop, February 25 1987.

20 *Sunday Express*, August 26 1984.

21 See G. Hodgson, *Lloyd's of London*, London, Penguin, 1986, p. 179.

22 Ibid., p. 192; *Ethnos*, May 20 1986; letter from Gillian Whitakker, March 6 1987; and interview with Barbara Conway, January 28 1987.

23 *Lloyd's List*, March 23 1985, p. 3 and February 14 1986, p. 1.

24 Ibid., January 16 1985, p. 1 and March 21 1985, p. 3.

25 Ibid., March 29 1985, p. 3, and G. Whitakker, 'Salem background', April 6 1985.

26 Ibid. and Whitakker letter, op.cit.

27 *Newsletter on the Oil Embargo Against South Africa*, vol. I, no. 2, June 1985, p. 4 and *The Times*, April 9 1985, p. 7.

28 *Lloyd's List*, May 20 1986, p. 1.

29 Ibid., February 1 1986, p. 3, February 13, p. 3 and February 14, p. 1; and 'Salem background', op. cit.

30 *Lloyd's List*, May 23 1986, p. 1, May 24, p. 1 and May 27, p. 1; and Whitakker letter, op. cit.

31 Government's Trial Memorandum, US District Court for the Southern District of Texas, Houston Division, *U.S. v. Soudan*, p. 2; M. Seward, 'Salem scam', *Oceans*, November 1985, p. 22; and *U.S. v. Soudan*, vol. I, p.44.

32 *Lloyd's List*, September 29 1984, p. 1 and October 24 1984, p. 1; *The Star*, October 8 1984; and Shorrock plea-bargain agreement,

June 29 1984, Exhibit 1417, *U.S. v. Soudan*, op. cit.

33 Ibid., vol. VI and N. Stancill, 'A disappearing act with a tanker filled with crude oil', *National Law Journal*, vol. 7, February 18 1985, p. 6.

34 Government's Trial Memorandum. op. cit., pp. 57-8.

35 *Financial Mail*, March 29 1985.

36 *Lloyd's List*, March 25 1985, p. 3.

37 See 'Maritime fraud', *Lloyd's Shipping Economist*, vol. 8, no. 2, February 1986, p. 9, and 'Judgment and Probation Commitment Order', U.S. District Court for the Southern District of Texas, Houston Division, May 3, 1985. It appears that at least $300,000 in compensation money was paid.

38 Comments on some legal interpretations related to the case appear in a letter from Peter Fishbein, January 27 1987.

39 *U.S. v. Soudan*, op. cit., vol. I, pp. 32-3 and Exhibits 1041 and 1064, ibid.

40 Two examples are the letters from Eric Ellen, Director of the International Maritime Bureau, April 11 1985 and Dr F.L. Wiswall Jr., Admiralty Counsel, Liberian Bureau of Maritime Affairs, New York office, April 9 1985.

41 See *Lloyd's List*, January 10 1985, p. 3.

42 *U.S. v. Soudan*, US Court of Appeals, Fifth Circuit, December 15, 1986, pp. 3033-6.

43 Ibid., p. 3037.

44 Ibid., pp. 3037-8.

45 Letter from Judge Bue, June 2 1987.

Assessing the Damage

1 J. Bologna, *Corporate Fraud*, Boston, Butterworth, 1984, pp. 2-3.

2 See ibid., pp. 16-17.

3 D.G. Powles and S.J. Hazelwood, 'Maritime fraud', *The Journal of Business Law*, September 1984, p. 407.

4 *Lloyd's List*, August 11 1983, p. 1.

5 IMCO, Twelfth Session, Assembly, November 1981, London, IMO, 1982, p. 395.

6 *Lloyd's List*, February 17 1984, p. 2, February 18, p. 1 and November 2 1985, p. 1.

7 Interview with Gerald Cooper, March 24 1987.

8 A. Tzamtzis, 'A marine fraud 2,350 years ago', *Naftiliaki*, January 1982, pp. 92-3.

■ Index